© 2012 OpenForum Europe LTD. and the respective authors of each chapter.

ISBN 978-1-300-17718-0

Edited by Shane Coughlan

The contents of this book are licensed under the Creative Commons Attribution-ShareAlike 3.0 Unported (CC BY-SA 3.0). Learn more here: http://creativecommons.org/licenses/by-sa/3.0/

Published by OpenForum Europe LTD for
OpenForum Academy

Table of Contents

Openness and Legitimacy in Standards Development
Andrew Updegrove   Page 5

Estimating the Economic Contribution of Open Source Software to the European Economy
Carlo Daffara   Page 11

IT usage in Swedish primary schools: Observations on Innovation and Educational Lock-In
Björn Lundell   Page 15

Unsettling Users: Openness and the Rise of Inverse Infrastructures
Tineke M. Egyedi and Wim Vree   Page 23

Copyright, Interfaces, and a Possible Atlantic Divide
Simonetta Vezzoso   Page 29

Framing the Conundrum of Total Cost of Ownership of Open Source Software
Maha Shaikh and Tony Cornford   Page 37

Consumer Trust, Education and Empowerment: The Open Story
Altsitsiadis Efthymios   Page 43

The Evolution Of Openness: Collaboration On Shared Platforms
Shane Coughlan   Page 49

Open Content Mining
Peter Murray-Rust, Jenny Molloy and Diane Cabell   Page 57

Complexities in the Relationship among Standarization, Invention and Innovation in Information and Communication Technologies: An introductory perspective
Jochen Friedrich   Page 65

About OpenForum Academy   Page 71
About OpenForum Europe   Page 73
Members of OpenForum Europe   Page 75
Mission, Policies and Code of Conduct   Page 76
Useful Links   Page 77
Further Reading on Openness   Page 78
Enter The Conversation (space for notes)   Page 79

Openness and Legitimacy in Standards Development

Andrew Updegrove
Founding Partner
Gesmer Updegrove LLP
United States of America
Andrew.Updegrove@gesmer.com

Abstract—Consensus regarding which specifications can rightfully claim to be "open standards" has been notably difficult to achieve in recent times. Usually, the question is academic, but when governments restrict their very substantial purchasing power to the acquisition of products and services implementing only such standards, then the selection of openness criteria can become contentious. In this article, I review traditional SDO and modern consortia norms of openness, as well as the standards related goals, and resulting definitions, of openness to be found in a variety of modern government and treaty formulations.

There is perhaps no phrase in standards development less susceptible to a common definition than the deceptively simple words, 'open standards.' A commonly expressed industry sentiment is that there can, and should, be no such common definition when it comes to rules relating to intellectual property rights included in such standards. Instead, it is said, 'openness' should be understood as a situation-specific waypoint located along a spectrum of multiple attributes and process requirements. Utilizing such a relativistic approach permits a balancing of factors in any given case, such as sectoral norms, stakeholder requirements, and market demands, to determine which processes and rules are essential and which might be superfluous, and even damaging. Even then, the list of elements that might (or in another person's opinion, might not) qualify as requirements can be both lengthy and the related discussions contentiousness.[1]

Differences in definitions for open standards might be accepted simply as an example of healthy market-based competition in business models (which indeed they are), but for the question of legitimacy in the eyes of third parties, and especially legitimacy for purposes of trade regulations and government procurement. If openness becomes a factor (as it has) in defining what standards do and do not qualify under relevant laws, regulations or international treaties, then the definition used necessarily takes on significant importance for commercial interests, and often for consumers and citizens as well.

In this article I will briefly review the historical evolution of open standards definitions, the manners in which they have become legally significant, and finally, current developments nationally, regionally and globally that touch upon this issue.

History of openness principles: The history of standards development in the modern era can be roughly divided into two periods. The first began in the late 19th century, and resulted in the gradual evolution of a two-tier, global development and acceptance infrastructure. The first tier was made up of national standards development organizations (SDOs), which were in turn represented in the second tier, comprising a small number of global non-government and treaty organizations, including the "Big Is" (ISO, IEC and ITU), within which the majority of internationally recognized standards were adopted. In the course of this evolution, a set of values and process expectations evolved that were agreed to represent baseline principles necessary to establish the legitimacy of the SDO, entitling its standards to be considered for acceptance on a global basis. These principles included process-oriented values such as accessibility to all affected stakeholders and transparency to non-participants, as well as fair competition concepts, such as the obligation to make available to all standards implementers any embedded intellectual property rights (principally patents) on fair, reasonable and non-discriminatory (FRAND) terms.

Each of these lofty principles was articulated in only a few words. Various supporting processes were designed at the national level to live up to the principles. The resulting activities were not supervised by the Big Is, because these organizations had no authority to review actions in member nations, no remit to accept appeals, and no powers of enforcement in the case of a failure by a member to adhere to standards of openness (a state of affairs that continues to exist today). But still, there was consensus on the principles, and

---

[1] A frequently cited (and extensive) list of attributes of openness has been assembled by Ken Krechmer. See, The Meaning of Open Standards, The International Journal of IT Standards and Standardization Research, Vol. 4 No. 1, January - June 2006, available at http://www.csrstds.com/openstds.pdf . Krechmer proposes that openness requirements should be assessed from the differing viewpoints of the implementers and users as well as the creators of standards, and then identifies ten categories under which openness criteria can be identified and organized.

consensus was, after all, one of the primary process values of the principles themselves.

The second era began in the early 1980s with the rise in the information technology (IT) sector of what are most commonly referred to today as consortia, beginning roughly in the early 1980s. These initiatives represented a move by industry to 'opt out' of the traditional SDO system, in part to assert more control, in part to limit development activities to their commercial peers, and in part to move more quickly from concept to standards implemented in actual products.

While vendors had always been the most directly interested and numerous participants in SDOs, companies in the rapidly evolving filed of computer technology increasingly chaffed under the often glacial process of the SDOs, encumbered in part by the delays that requirements to achieve consensus and to provide a right of appeal imposed, especially when enabled through procedural steps in a pre-Internet world dependent on face to face meetings and surface mail. Over time, the great majority of information technology, and to a lesser extent communications technology, standards development opted out of the world of SDOs. In a rather Orwellian sense, the animals in the land of information and communications (ICT) had evicted the farmers, and taken over the farm.

These new consortia were typically narrow in focus (often developing a single standard), industry driven, and (if they so desired) unencumbered by the principles of the past. They were also vigorously goal oriented – with the goal being wide spread adoption of a standard rather than simply its development. Accordingly, they took on such additional activities as might be necessary in the given case to achieve that goal, including promotion, test suite development, certification and branding programs, and much more.

But over time, a strange process began to unfold: the animals began to look more like the farmers, as some consortia broadened their scope, and others were founded to serve as centers of development in their self-assigned domains, becoming not unlike the many scores of SDOs formed in the U.S., each to serve the standards needs of a discrete market sector. Unlike these SDOs, however, consortia almost always aspired to international membership, and to the direct adoption of their standards on a global basis. Most significantly for current purposes, consortia also started to adopt most (but not all) of the same principles that had become normative in the traditional world of standards development.

That this should occur is not surprising. While traditional principles, as a lawyer might observe, 'sound in equity,' in fact, they are equally justifiable from the perspective of self-interest, because standards uptake is by definition voluntary (except when a standard is referenced into law). Absent the kind of market power in a standards development group that leaves the marketplace no choice but to adopt, consortia as well as SDOs are wise to pledge allegiance to, and also implement, the type of process and procedures that can assure everyone that they would be safer and smarter to participate in the development and adoption of a new standard than to stand aside and reject the specification in question.

An excellent way to convince competitors that a given initiative represents an opportunity rather than a threat can be found in honoring and implementing principles such as open participation (so that all can affect the result) and transparency (so that all can see that games are not being played, and expose them if they are). So it came to pass that those who formed consortia began to consciously design their governance structures and processes to demonstrate and guarantee that these principles would be protected in the breach.

That said, a one to one correspondence did not come to exist between the principles espoused by SDOs and those which guide consortia. For example, in SDOs, achieving consensus typically involves recording, responding to, and reconciling objections of dissenting participants in a working group, and a formal appeals process. Consortia, true to the original goals of their creators, are likely to adopt more agile, real time (rather than necessarily sequential, and therefore time consuming) mechanisms that nonetheless satisfy member-perceived requirements for due process.

Moreover, over time additional developments in the ICT sector introduced new standards-relevant differentiators from the traditional standards development sector, and this process has accelerated. Chief among them have been the advent of the Internet and the Web, each supported by a strong culture of 'free,' the rise of open source software, often made available under license terms incompatible with RAND declarations, and a remarkable convergence of technologies in laptops and mobile devices, resulting not uncommonly in the implementation of many hundreds of standards in a single device.[2] The market-based expectations resulting from these developments have led many consortia to alter their intellectual property rights (IPR) rules and processes in response.

Trade Regulation and Government Procurement: At the same time that matters were changing at both traditional and modern setting organizations (SSOs), rules were developing, and then coming under stress, within government circles.

---

[2] Brad Biddle, with co-authors Sean Wood and Andrew White have concluded that a typical laptop implements at least 251 interoperability standards alone, with the total number of included standards being far higher. See, How Many Standards in a Laptop? (and other Empirical Questions), available at: http://standardslaw.org/How_Many_Standards.pdf

Perhaps not surprisingly, these rules initially recapitulated the principles of openness that had evolved within the traditional world of SDOs, and not the ever changing landscape upon which consortia are active. Indeed, when there were only 'de facto' standards owned by individual companies and 'de jure' standards owned by SDOs, it was easier for governments to simply require the implementation of standards developed by SDOs than to delve into definitions of openness.

Europe: This was the route pursued in the European Union, where the only standards eligible for referencing in government procurement came from recognized global SDOs, such as the Big Is, and Europe's own regional SDOs (CEN, CENELEC and ETSI, organizations developing 'European Standards' under mandates from the EU). In recent years in the ICT sector, however, it has become clear that a rigid commitment to such a rule flies in the face of reality, given the pervasiveness of consortium-developed standards in most key areas of ICT.

This uncomfortable truth was recognized in one of the ten recommendations made in the 2010 Report of the Export Panel for the Review of the European Standardization System (ESS), which stated that:

> ...in many areas there is pressure for fora and consortia specifications to be "recognized" in some way, and to facilitate the uptake of such specifications in a public policy or public procurement context. It is proposed that... the ESS will ensure that it has the improved mechanisms to interact with fora and consortia and ensure that the best standards are adopted appropriately.

Since the date of this report, the EU has moved (not without much *sturm und drang*) gradually in this direction, and regulations are now being formulated that are expected to act on this recommendation, although the final details are as yet unknown.

Meanwhile, a more long-standing debate regarding the use of standards by government continues in Europe, this one focusing expressly on 'openness.' This dialogue was occasioned by the development by the European Commission of a European Interoperability Framework (EIF) for Pan-European eGovernment Services, the first version of which was released in 2004.[3] The reason that standards were to be independently addressed in this context relates to the purpose of the Framework, which is, to "support the delivery of pan-European eGovernment services to citizens and enterprises." Issues such as accessibility (both physical and economic) and technology neutrality were therefore recognized as being of special concern.

The first version of the Framework adopted the use of 'Open Standards' as an underlying principle, and established four 'minimal characteristics' for such standards:

[1] The standard is adopted and will be maintained by a not-for-profit organisation, and its ongoing development occurs on the basis of an open decision-making procedure available to all interested parties (consensus or majority decision etc.).
[2] The standard has been published and the standard specification document is available either freely or at a nominal charge. It must be permissible to all to copy, distribute and use it for no fee or at a nominal fee.
[3] The intellectual property - i.e. patents possibly present - of (parts of) the standard is made irrevocably available on a royalty free basis.
[4] There are no constraints on the re-use of the standard.

This definition was notable – and controversial – for a variety of reasons. First, it expressed no preference for the output of SDOs. Second, it acknowledged that some traditional indicia of openness might not be uniquely desirable after all (e.g., majority voting could be an acceptable alternative to consensus). Next, it cut to the root of the largest source of income upon which many SDOs rely (SDOs typically charge a significant fees to purchase a single, non-distributable copy of their standards; virtually all consortia, on the other hand, make their standards available for free). Lastly, and most controversially, owners of patent claims that would be necessarily infringed by implementation of a standard would be barred from charging a royalty.

Following aggressive lobbying by multiple constituencies, the definition was substantially diluted in Version 2.0 of the Framework (now titled the European Framework for European public Services), which was released in December, 2010.[4] In this version, the EIF no longer speaks in terms of minimum requirements at all, nor does it include the use of Open Standards as an 'underlying principle' (although values such as Openness and Transparency do apply with respect to the Framework generally). Instead, it only observes that, "The level of openness of a formalised specification is an important element in determining the possibility of sharing and reusing software components implementing that specification," and noting that:

> If the openness principle is applied in full:
>
> • All stakeholders have the same possibility of contributing to the development of the

---

[3] http://ec.europa.eu/idabc/servlets/Docd552.pdf?id=19529

[4] http://ec.europa.eu/isa/documents/isa_annex_ii_eif_en.pdf

2. specification and public review is part of the decision-making process;
3. The specification is available for everybody to study;
4. Intellectual property rights related to the specification are licensed on FRAND19 terms or on a royalty-free basis in a way that allows implementation in both proprietary and open source software.

The single Recommendation (number 22) in EIF 2.0 that mentions 'open standards' (as compared to simply 'specifications') reads as follows: "When establishing European public services, public administrations should prefer open specifications, taking due account of the coverage of functional needs, maturity and market support."[5] Nevertheless, even in its current, diluted form, the absence of any reference at all to Big I standards is remarkable, given the equally vigorous debate that is still ongoing in the EU regarding the legitimacy of SDO vs. consortium developed standards in public procurement generally, more than eight years after the release of the initial version of the EIF.

World Trade Organization: A quite different approach was taken under the WTO's Agreement on Technical Barriers to Trade (ATBT).[6] This is hardly surprising, because the ATBT is focused on preventing standards-based trade gamesmanship, rather than caring about the quality or development mode of standards as such. The primary standards-related directive, found in Article 2, Section 2.4 reads as follows:

> Where technical regulations are required and relevant international standards exist or their completion is imminent, Members shall use them, or the relevant parts of them, as a basis for their technical regulations except when such international standards or relevant parts would be an ineffective or inappropriate means for the fulfillment of the legitimate objectives pursued,…

Article 4 of the Act requires that the domestic SDOs of signatory nations must, "adopt and comply with" a Code of Good Practice that is appended to the ATBT as Annex 3. The terms of the Code of Good Practice do include some requirements relating to open participation and transparency, but the context makes it clear that the intention relates not to values-based principles, but to drive national efforts towards, "harmonizing standards on as wide a basis as possible." Perhaps due to the focus of the WTO on actions by signatory parties, the requirements of the main text of the ATBT as well as that of the Annex, are addressed only to SDOs that are national or regional in scope.

Global consortia are therefore definitionally excluded as objects of national signatory obligations. Lastly, it should be noted that the ATBT speaks only of "international standards" rather than referring to the origin of such standards. In other words, the WTO takes a substantially neutral position on how standards are created, except to the extent that their mode of creation leads to a harmonized global marketplace. The ATBT is also silent with respect to whether the Code of Good Practices should be adopted by consortia, although standards that have achieved global adoption would appear to enjoy equal status under the ATBT, whether developed by SDOs or consortia.

United States: The United States has taken an approach with respect to procurement regulations that is at once more granular relating to the definition of open standards than EIF 2.0 but similarly tepid regarding the degree of preference to be given to open standards, other than (impliedly) where there are two equally viable alternatives from which to choose.

The rationale of the U.S. definition can be found in the fact that in 1995 Congress dictated that government should get out of the business of developing, and requiring compliance with, 'government unique' standards. That directive was set forth in the Technology Transfer and Advancement Act,[7] which was subsequently augmented by Office of Management and Budget Circular A-119.[8]

Circular A-119 uses the term 'voluntary consensus standards' instead of 'open standards.' It defines such standards as follows:

> a. For purposes of this policy, "voluntary consensus standards" are standards developed or adopted by voluntary consensus standards bodies, both domestic and international. These standards include provisions requiring that

---

[5] For a more in depth analysis of the changes between the two versions of the EIF, see, Updegrove, Andrew, EC Takes One Step Forward, Two Steps Back, ConsortiumInfo.org Standards Blog (December 21, 2010), at: http://www.consortiuminfo.org/standardsblog/article.php?story=20101221084910541

[6] http://www.wto.org/english/docs_e/legal_e/17-tbt.pdf

[7] National Technology Transfer and Advancement Act of 1995, 15 U.S.C. § 3701 (1995), available at http://ftp.resource.org/gpo.gov/laws/104/publ113.104.txt

[8] OMB Circular A-119 Revised, Federal Participation in the Development and Use of Voluntary Consensus Standards and in Conformity Assessment Activities (rev. Feb. 10, 1998), available at http://www.whitehouse.gov/omb/rewrite/circulars/a119/a119.html

owners of relevant intellectual property have agreed to make that intellectual property available on a non-discriminatory, royalty-free or reasonable royalty basis to all interested parties....

(1) "Voluntary consensus standards bodies" are domestic or international organizations which plan, develop, establish, or coordinate voluntary consensus standards using agreed-upon procedures....A voluntary consensus standards body is defined by the following attributes:

    (i) Openness.
    (ii) Balance of interest.
    (iii) Due process.
    (vi) An appeals process.
    (v) Consensus, which is defined as general agreement, but not necessarily unanimity, and includes a process for attempting to resolve objections by interested parties, as long as all comments have been fairly considered, each objector is advised of the disposition of his or her objection(s) and the reasons why, and the consensus body members are given an opportunity to change their votes after reviewing the comments.

While the OMB definition of voluntary consensus standards borrows heavily on the traditional process and IPR focused rules of SDOs, the last attribute of the definition leaps out due to its great level of detail. The particularity of this criterion, in contrast to those that precede it (each of which could have been expanded to a similar degree) apparently arose from a desire to mimic to the extent possible the protections inherent in the U.S. administrative law adoption process. This was felt to be necessary by those that drafted the definition due to the fact that Congress was, in effect, delegating a significant governmental function to the private sector.[9]

While Circular A-119 gives Federal agencies substantial leeway regarding which private sector standards they may choose to utilize, it is regrettable that such a granular approach was taken regarding the definition of voluntary consensus standards, due to the fact that, as earlier noted, the marketplace has found that equally efficacious and less burdensome processes can be used to create robust, open, and widely adopted standards.[10]

Conclusions: It is likely that governments and industry will continue to struggle with definitions of open standards. Indeed, in August of this year, several of the SSOs that have been most influential in the development of the standards enabling the Internet and the Web issued their own set of principles for standards development. A significant motivation for this initiative appears to be an effort to claim equal legitimacy with the Big Is in the run up to a meeting of the ITU-T this December, at which (it is rumored) the ITU-T intends to seek to wrest a degree of control over the Internet away from the SSOs that have helped to make it what it is today. While reminiscent of traditional tenets, the elements underlying the principles endorsed by the group of SSOs include some intriguing additions that are in some ways reflective of modern realities, and in others serving the purposes of the organizations involved in making the joint announcement.[11][12]

In light of the situational differences between industry sectors and standards applications, and between the disparate goals of governments and treaty organizations, it would seem that there is some validity to the industry contention that the importance of some elements of open standards definitions (e.g., relating to intellectual property rights) should in some cases be evaluated on a situational basis. Most obviously, the relevance to the public of the technical parameters of an obscure widget in the electronic bowels of a server is far different from the public interest in an accessibility standard to be universally deployed at government Web sites.[13] Process controls that

---

[9] Personal communication with James H. Turner, Jr., former Chief Counsel of the U.S. House of Representatives Committee on Science and Technology, who was directly involved in the drafting of the Act.

[10] The Department of Commerce recently invited the submission of comments relating to the Circular which may lead to its amendment, or more likely the release of additional guidance to the Federal agencies in respect of its implementations. My written comments, presented verbally at a government workshop, can be found at https://law.resource.org/pub/us/cfr/regulations.gov.docket.02/09000064810013ef.pdf

[11] The principles can be found at: http://open-stand.org/principles/ For a detailed analysis, see, Leading Standards Organizations Assert Principles of a "New Global Standards Paradigm," Updegrove, Andrew, ConsortiumInfo.org Standards Blog (August 30, 2012), at: http://www.consortiuminfo.org/standardsblog/article.php?story=20120830102530600

[12] While definitions are helpful, confirmation is another matter. I have proposed that the creation of a global entity capable of certifying compliance with open standards development processes would be useful. See, A Proposal for a New Type of Global Standards Certification, Standards Today (Vol. VI, No. 8), Oct. – Nov. 2007, available at:

[13] I have forcefully argues for the recognition of what I refer to as "Civil ICT Standards," and for the protections that should be

would be relevant to the adoption of the latter would impose needless burdens on the creation of the former, because the public would not avail itself of the opportunities to participate or comment in any event. On the other hand, the creation of such a widget remains of significant importance from the perspective of antitrust and trade laws.

At the end of the day, if governments wish to adopt minimum requirements (or, more realistically, preferences) – as they should, in the appropriate situation - what is needed is not a simplistic one size fits all solution, but a more nuanced approach that recognizes the following:

1. A base level of important openness elements (e.g., participation, transparency, availability, consensus/majority, technology neutrality) that should be regarded as applicable to the processes and other attributes of all types of standards, taking competition and trade law concerns into account.

2. Special requirements that map to the unique needs of discrete situations and/or policy goals, such as mandating elements appropriate to protect civil rights exercised electronically.

3. The means to enable implementation of standards in both open source as well as proprietary software.

If such a relative approach is followed in ICT, it should be possible to ensure that those openness attributes that are appropriate and important will be employed when they are necessary, and not where their imposition would only tax a process that provides value as much based on agility and speed as on technical merit.

---

afforded to their development and adoption. See, for example, http://www.consortiuminfo.org/bulletins/feb08.php#feature

Estimating the Economic Contribution of Open Source Software to the European Economy

Carlo Daffara
CloudWeavers UK
carlo.daffara@cloudweavers.eu

Abstract—There have been several research efforts in the past that tried to assess the real value introduced in the EU economy through the adoption of Open Source Software, with inconclusive results. A different approach based on collated data from several code reuse surveys, coupled with a set of macroeconomic estimates provide an indication of savings for the EU economy of at least 114B€/year, not including second order effects. *(Abstract)*

Index Terms—**Open Source, Economics.** *(key words)*

I. INTRODUCTION: MEASUREMENT APPROACHES

What is the real value that Open Source has brought to the economy? This is not a peregrine question. Since most of the current evaluation methods are based on assessing "sales", that is direct monetization of OSS, we are currently missing from this view the large, mostly under-reported and underestimated aspect of open source use that is not "sold", but for example is directly introduced through an internal work force, or in services, or embedded inside an infrastructure. Estimating the savings or the economic benefit that the EU economy as a whole receives from OSS is for this reason extremely difficult.

A first approach based on measuring directly the so called "OSS economy", that is the firms that identify themselves as providing Open Source Services or software through one of several business models [1] falls short of measuring contributions from companies where such a monetization is ancillary to a separate market, for example hardware or software services. An example of the problems related to this method is apparent in the discrepancy between a measured worldwide OSS industry value of 8B€ in 2008 [2] compared with the fact that in 2005 HP reported Linux-related revenues higher than 2.5B$, or that IBM in the same year reported OSS-related revenues of 4.5B$. Even niche markets, like the market for OSS PBX systems [3] was reported to be bigger than 1.2B$ in 2008, making it clear that the OSS industry value largely underestimates the economic value of contributions from companies that do not identify themselves as "OSS companies". Not only does this approach underestimate the market, it totally ignores the work that is performed without a monetary compensation and it under-reports the software that is distributed widely from a single source (for example, the open source code that is embedded in phones or routers).

An alternative and apparently easy approach - called "substitution principle" - tries to measure how much a collection of hard-to-measure assets is valued by counting the sum of the money necessary to substitute them; for example, counting the value of all the Apache web servers by adding the cost of changing them all with an average marketed substitute.

An example of such an approach was a set of estimates from the Standish Group: "First we listed the major open source products. Then we looked at the commercial equivalents. Next we looked at the average cost of both the open source products and the commercial products, giving us a net commercial cost. We then multiplied the net cost of the commercial product by our open source shipping estimates." This is similar to the approach used by copyright enforcement agencies to estimate piracy losses - by counting how many times the copy of a film is downloaded, and assuming that all the people that downloaded it would have paid for a full cinema ticket if piracy did not exist, an assumption that is not compatible with known data.

This approach is however highly unreliable for two reasons: first of all, it introduces a strong bias related to the fact that software is never perfectly exchangeable with an alternative. Claiming that pricing is equivalent when the product is not introduces an error that increases with the degree of non-substitutability of a product (for example, LibreOffice may be perceived as sometimes incompatible with other proprietary office productivity suites, and as such it may be perceived as a partial substitute only). The second is related to the fact that users may be unwilling to pay for an alternative, or would not have adopt it in the first place had it been not free. In this sense, claiming that the economic value of a product like the Apache web server is the same of the equivalent leading proprietary web server implies that if Apache did not exist, the users would have paid for and used the proprietary replacement, while some may have decided to not use a web server at all – making the comparison useless.

II. ESTIMATING CODE REUSE

A different approach may be to infer the savings from data that is related to the degree of reuse of OSS, starting from the macroeconomic view. To avoid underestimation, we will start from the inclusive market view of all the IT sector, valued in 2010 at 624B€ worldwide; of this EU27 represents 35%, for a total of 224B€ [2]. This estimate however ignores the economic equivalent of effort created by employees that work in ICT but are not employed as IT personnel, a substantial percentage of the overall workforce. To take into account such an "hidden" value, we can use a macroeconomic data from Gartner [4] that estimates at 4% the percentage of investment that is directly or indirectly imputable to IT. Using this data at the EU macro level and using the 2010 GDP, we can estimate at 374B€ the total value of the IT market including the internal effort of companies and public administrations [5]

A parallel estimate using collective data from IT industry association around the world provided by WITSA [6] provides (after removing communications and hardware from the total value) an estimate for the EU market of 399B€, in line with our previous computation.

Removing from this value the effort for user support, training and other ancillary services (including financial services) we reach a software-related total economic value of 244B€/year. This market is substantially larger than the traditional "shrinkwrapped" software, that is software that is designed and developed to be sold – according to the FISTERA thematic network and Gosh [7], such market is 19% of the total, while OECD reports 26%[8] like PAC [2] - in any case substantially smaller than the rest, composed of internal and custom development by third parties.

A substantial percentage of this software is actually Open Source – a fact that applies both to internally developed software and contracted development. In fact, several sources report substantial quantities of code reused:

- Black Duck: "The results revealed that an average product or application contains almost 700 MB of code, 22% of which is open source software ... almost 80% of newly deployed code is Open Source" [9]
- The Koders survey in 2010 found that 44% of all code was Open Source [5]
- Sojer and Henkel reported a share of 30% of code reused among the surveyed projects [10]
- Veracode: "sampling continues to find that between 30 and 70% of code submitted as Internally Developed is identifiably from third-parties, most often in the form of Open Source components and Commercial libraries" [11]
- Gartner reported that among the surveyed customers, 26% of the code deployed was Open Source [12]

By taking into account the observation that use of OSS code increases with time – with more recent development reusing a higher share of code from open projects – we can estimate that 35% of the code that was overall deployed in the last 5 years is actually directly or indirectly derived from Open Source.

To provide an indication of the savings introduced by this reuse process, we will leverage a preexisting model of code cost estimation called COCOMOII, adapted for the specifics of Open Source reuse [13]. The model is based on a set of different cost estimates for separate part of the project:

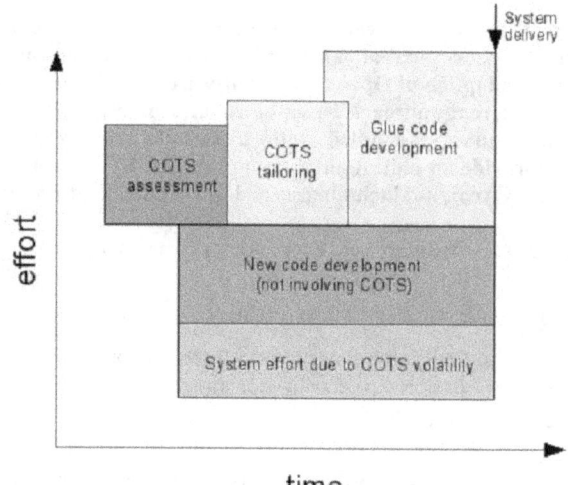

The model, due to Bohem [14] takes into account the fact that reusing external resources (called "COTS", for Commercial Off The Shelf) introduces both savings due to the reduced development effort but some costs as well – specifically a variable cost related to the increased risk due to the lack of control of an external resource like the OSS project itself, and tailoring and "glue code" development necessary to adapt and integrate the software component with the rest of the code. Using the adapted model[1] a summary table of the results is:

Project size (code lines)	% of OSS	total cost (Keuro)	Savings	duration (years)	avg. staffing
100000	0	1703	0%	1.7	20.5
100000	50	975	43%	1.3	15.4
100000	75	487	71%	0.9	8.6
1000000	0	22000	0%	3.3	141.7
1000000	50	12061	45%	2.6	103.2
1000000	75	3012	86%	2	32
10000000	0	295955	0%	7.5	818
10000000	50	160596	46%	5.9	631.2
10000000	75	80845	73%	3.8	421

---

[1] The model uses a percentage of 15% of code tailored, with a complexity index of 6 compared with new code development. Volatility is approximated with an average additional effort of 1.5 to 2.5 full-time person-year.

If we add to the costs related to reuse the effort necessary to identify and select the OSS components to be reused (the so called "search cost") we can estimate that the total savings attributable to a 35% reuse are equivalent to 31% of total coding effort, for a first order savings of 75B€/year.

This is however only a small part of the real impact of this specific form of reuse. Additional savings are also imputable to the improvement in success rate, reduction of maintenance costs and time to market - and the especially important effect of reinvestment of savings into new IT developments.

The success rate of IT projects is highly dependent on the size of the project itself and the effort, with a substantial percentage of project delayed or canceled [15] - a fact that introduces a sort of "failure tax" on all developments. A survey of success rate for projects of different sizes is summarized as follows:

size	People	Time	success rate
< 750K$	6	6	55%
750K to 1.5M	12	9	33%
1.5M to 3M	25	12	25%
3 to 6	40	18	15%
6 to 10	250+	24+	8%
>10M	500+	36+	0%

The data on canceled projects is abundant, and as an excerpt:

- Jones [16] reports that "the cancellation rate for applications in the 10,000 function point size range is about 31%. The average cost for these cancelled projects is about $35,000,000"
- Standish group, 2009: 24% of projects are canceled before deployment [15]
- Sauer & Cuthbertson, in an Oxford university survey of 2003 [15]: 10%
- Dynamic Markets Limited [17]: 25%+ of all software and services projects are canceled before completion
- Dr Dobbs survey of IT project success [18]: Agile projects: 60% are successful, 28% are challenged, and 12% are failures; while for traditional projects: 47% are successful, 36% are challenged, and 17% are failures.

How does code reuse impact the project success rates? By reducing effort, staffing and duration the 35% code reuse introduces a reduction on these parameters of 10%, equivalent to a reduction in the failure rate of 2%, with an economic impact of 4.9B€ minimum.

Another important aspect is connected with maintenance costs: code that is reused is substantially better in terms of quality, a fact first observed by Mohageghi, Conrad and Schwarz [19]: the code that is reused (like Open Source code) improves faster and with substantially less effort than code that is not shared; its maintenance effort is also substantially lower than the average [20]. If we adopt the model by Jones and Bonsignour, traditional code does have a cost of 2000$ per function point, while code shared or developed using best practices has a lower cost of 1200$ per function point [16]. Using this values, the shared code in a reused OSS project introduces an additional reduction in maintenance and development of 14%, equivalent to an additional 34B€/year in savings.

III. REINVESTMENT EFFECTS

An especially important effect is the reinvestment of these savings into IT itself – a fact that can be verified by observing that the percentage of IT investment does not decrease, even when the percentage of OSS increases [6], a sign that savings are reinvested in the same sector. These investments are from a productivity point of view nearly neutral in the short term, with data from Brynjolfsson that indicates that: "The principal results from this econometric analysis are [that] the measured output contribution of computerization in the short-run are approximately equal to computer capital costs ..[and that] the measured long-run contributions of computerization are significantly above computer capital costs (a factor of five or more in point estimates." [21]

As the companies that use larger shares of OSS take advantage in a more extensive way of such output contribution, we can speculate that such companies should have a productivity or efficiency advantage over their peers. In fact, a study by VIU showed that: "… comparing the individual data on firms with turnover of less than 500,000 euros with the variable on size classes of customers (by number of employees), one can hypothesize a correlation between the use of software Open Source and the ability to attract customers of relatively larger scale. At the same turnover, in other words, companies 'Open Source only' seem to have more chances to obtain work orders from companies with more than 50 employees (ie medium – large compared to our universe of reference)." [5] Similar higher efficiency was found in OSS-intensive firms, with a 221% revenue per employee rating compared to the industry average [7]. We are thus justified in our hypothesis of the effect of higher efficiency due to the reinvestment of savings; by using the data from Brynjolfsson we can thus estimate a long term result in productivity and efficiency improvement that is (using an annualized, incremental model of return of invested capital) at a minimum equivalent to 342B€/year in added economic value.

IV. CONCLUSIONS

The data collected up to now indicates that Open Source does have at least an immediate economic effect through code reuse and effort reduction; a lower bound of such effects can be estimated to be at least 114B€/year, through direct savings, reduction in project failure and improvements in code maintenance costs - equivalent to 30% of the entire software and services market. Also, the effect of reinvestment of such savings into internal IT provides an additional second order effect in terms of productivity and increased efficiency of at least 342B€/year – a decidedly not marginal contribution to the European Economy.

REFERENCES

[1] Daffara, C. "Business models in Open Source companies" In: Workshop presentation at the 3rd Conference on Open Source Systems (OSS 2007).

[2] Pierre Audouin Consultants, "Economic and Social Impact of Software & Software-Based Services", EU Smart 2009/0041.

[3] Eastern Management Group, Open Source PBX: Market Size, Forecast and Analysis", 2010.

[4] Gartner Group, IT spending survey 2010

[5] Daffara, C. "The Economic Value of Open Source Software". Submitted presentation, TransferSummit Oxford 2010

[6] WITSA "DigitalPlanet 2010" report, retrived from http://www.witsa.org/v2/media_center/pdf/DP2010_ExecSumm_Final_LoRes.pdf

[7] Gosh et al., "Economic impact of open source software

[8] on innovation and the competitiveness of the

[9] Information and Communication Technologies

[10] (ICT) sector in the EU – Final report". UNU-Merit and European Commission, 2006

[11] Oecd, "The software sector: a statistical profile for selected oecd countries", 1998.

[12] McQuaide, B., "Distributed Multi-Source Development with Open Source:", LinuxCon 2010.

[13] Sojer M., Henkel J., "Code Reuse in Open Source Software Development: Quantitative Evidence, Drivers, and Impediments" Journal of the Association for Information Systems Special Issue on Empirical Research on Free/Libre Open Source Software Volume 11, Issue 11 (2010)

[14] Veracode, "State of Software Security Report volume 3", 2011

[15] Gartner group, "Overview of preferences and practices in the Adoption and Usage of Open Source Software", 2011

[16] Daffara, C. "Estimating savings from OSS code reuse, or: where does the money comes from?", 2011. Retrieved from http://carlodaffara.conecta.it/estimating-savings-from-oss-code-reuse-or-where-does-the-money-comes-from/

[17] Basili V.R., Bohem B., "COTS-based systems top 10 list", Computer, 2001

[18] Emam K.E., Koru A., "A replicated survey of IT Software project failure", IEEE Software, 2008

[19] Jones C., Bonsignour O., "The economics of software quality". Addison Wesley, 2012

[20] Dynamic Markets Limited, "IT Projects: Experience Certainty." Independent Market Research Report. August 2007.

[21] Dr Dobbs, "2010 IT Project Success Rates". Retrieved from http://www.drdobbs.com/architecture-and-design/2010-it-project-success-rates/226500046

[22] Mohagheghi P., Conradi R., Killi O.M., Schwarz H. "An Empirical Study of Software Reuse vs. Defect-Density and Stability", 2004. In Proceedings of the 26th International Conference on Software Engineering (ICSE '04)

[23] Capra E., Francalanci C., Merlo F., "The Economics of Community Open Source Software Projects: An Empirical Analysis of Maintenance Effort". Advances in Software Engineering - Special issue on new generation of software metrics archive, January 2010

[24] Brynjolfsson, E., and Hitt, L., "Beyond the productivity Paradox", Communications of the ACM, 1998

IT Usage in Swedish Primary Schools:

Observations on Innovation and Educational Lock-In

Björn Lundell
University of Skövde
Skövde, Sweden
bjorn.lundell@his.se

Abstract—We report on initial results from a survey conducted for establishing the state-of-practice with respect to student's IT usage in Swedish primary schools. There are a number of innovative efforts concerning IT usage, but students in many primary schools are also exposed to a number of different lock-in effects, including educational lock-in. Results reveal significant misconceptions concerning Open Source software and also considerable confusion amongst respondents related to the difference between software application and file format. The study characterises problems and provide recommended actions.

Index Terms—IT usage, primary schools, Open Source software, Open Standards, educational lock-in, survey.

I. Introduction

In this paper we report on results from an ongoing study aimed to establish the state of practice concerning IT usage in Swedish public sector primary and secondary schools. The paper presents initial results from an analysis of primary schools (ages 7-16) and is specifically focused on results regarding requirements for students related to: use of document formats (standards), applications for writing essays, and provision of IT equipment to students. Our analysis identifies a number of different types of lock-in effects, and specifically focuses on educational lock-in and discusses its potential implications in a long-term perspective.

Previous studies identified a number of challenges related to standardisation, public sector procurement, and lock-in [2] [8] [10] [11] [14] [15] [19]. In addition, there is a complex relationship between ICT standardisation and public procurement, with associated risks for different types of lock-in effects that can have severe consequences for different stakeholder groups [15]. Further, it has been noted that the "single-vendor 'solution', whether based on open or de facto standards, is a fairly widespread defensive procurement strategy." [5]

The inherent complexity in the link between ICT standardisation and public sector procurement is identified in DAE [3], and its policy actions include efforts aimed to improve public sector's use of standards which "can be implemented by all interested suppliers" in order to allow "for more competition and reduced risk of lock-in." [3]

In fact, one of its missions is to issue a communication that will "provide guidance on the link between ICT standardisation and public procurement to help public authorities to use standards to promote efficiency and reduce lock-in" [3], and results from a study of procurement practices in the EU have recently been published in order to provide guidance for an improved public sector procurement practice and an improved ICT standardisation for Europe [8]. From this, and previous studies, we conclude that many practitioners seem unaware of fundamental concepts and their implications for practice in this area.

Further, skills development in the ICT have sector been identified as important, not only for public sector procurement and standardisation, but also for a range of different stakeholder groups. We note that the European Commission reports, in its annual scoreboard, that "sufficient ICT skills" is an area of major concern as half of "European labour force does not have sufficient ICT skills to help them change or find a new job." [4]

In summary, there seems to be an urgent need for an improved practice which requires competences and and skills development for different stakeholder groups in the ICT area in general, and specifically related to public sector procurement, use of standards, and strategies for how to address risks associated with different types of lock-in.

One important aspect of such skills development concerns lock-in related to educational contexts in public sector schools. This is an important dimension for the analysis of the results from the study reported on in this paper. To date, there is limited research reporting on educational lock-in and use of standards related to IT usage in public sector schools.

II. On openness and IT usage in Swedish primary schools

For a number of years, the Swedish governments and individual spokespersons have expressed support for an increased openness (in general) in society, and several such statements have more specifically concerned IT usage with policy statements related to Open Standards and Open Source software.

For example, in its 2004 IT bill (2004/05:175), the Swedish government declared that the use of Open Standards and Open Source software should be promoted [7]. More recently, in a public speech on innovations for Europe during the Swedish EU presidency, the responsible minister presented the Swedish position on the importance of openness in the public sector:

"It is my belief that we need a clear definition of openness in the European Interoperability Framework and that the definition of open standards and open source software as defined by the European Interoperability Framework version one has served us well so far. The use of open standards and open source solutions decreases the public sector's reliance on specific vendors and platforms and it increases European competitiveness as well as the transparency" [17]

Further, the concept of Open Standard has been clarified in the Swedish context through inclusion of a clear definition of openness (adopted from the EIF version one) in the first report from the Swedish e-Governance initiative [22]. With the clarification of this fundamental concept, important principles underlying the idea of an Open Standard has been established.

First, use of an Open Standard ensures that data and systems can be interpreted independently of the tool which generated it, something which is particularly important in an educational context as students cannot be expected to buy (or pay for renting) specific proprietary technology when studying in Swedish primary schools. In fact, the The Swedish Schools Inspectorate examines an important principle for education in Sweden, namely that "education shall be free of charge" [21]. Further, [21] clarifies that costs for calculators used in primary schools and costs related to use and insurances of laptops provided (free of charge) to students for use at school and at home cannot be charged for. However, a minor fee (approx. €10) can be accepted on an occasional basis, such as for costs related to a day with outdoor activities.

Second, an Open Standard [6] [22] is a standard which has certain open properties. When a standard is published and its technical specification contains sufficiently detailed information it can be used as a basis for implementation in software systems under different proprietary licenses and different Open Source software licenses. With Open Standards as a basis for procurement of IT, software systems, and educational (digital) learning objects (i.e. educational material, documents, and data which are maintained in Open Standards) in an educational context, there will be reduced risks for discrimination against students and more alternatives for potential adoption and use (since Open Standards can be implemented in software licensed under both proprietary and Open Source software licenses). Such a strategy is well in line with a statement from Kroes, then European Commissioner for Competition Policy, in a public speech: "No citizen or company should be forced or encouraged to use a particular company's technology to access government information." [13]

More recently, the Swedish minister responsible for IT, has organised a set of round-table discussions concerning IT and the Digital Agenda for Sweden, and as part of this covered the topic IT usage in schools and education [16]. In a public speech, she notes that many schools provide IT equipment to their students, but also stresses: "I would argue that for schools there is much room for improvement in terms of IT use." [12]

Such a view is, perhaps, not surprising in light of recent statistics reported by the Swedish National Agency for Education based on their survey results regarding primary schools [20]. Their results show that computers are most commonly used when teaching the subject Swedish (as a native language) with students aged 13 to 15 years old. For this group of students, results for computer usage when teaching Swedish show that 17% of the students "never" and 32% "rarely" use computers, which imply that almost half (49%) of Swedish students rarely or never use computers. It should be noted that writing essays and reports are rather common activities in primary schools, and in light of these results, statements concerning room for improvements in terms of use of IT by the Swedish IT-minister may, perhaps, not be perceived as surprising.

Further, according to the chair for the educational commission at Swedish Association of Local Authorities and Regions (SALAR) most students learn IT at home with associated risks for a digital divide and that there is an urgent need for an IT-strategy for Swedish schools and IT competence in schools [18]. Similarly, according to the managing director for UR, the Swedish Educational Broadcasting Company, there is currently an absurd lack of computers in the Swedish classrooms [9]. However, there are also more positive reports from schools. For example, by adoption of Open Source software solutions a public sector school was able to significantly reduce costs at a range which made it possible to provide one computer per student instead of six to seven students per computer within the same total budget [1].

III. RESEARCH APPROACH

Our goal is to establish the state of practice concerning IT usage in Swedish public sector primary and secondary schools, and to address this a survey was designed in order to collect responses from all public sector primary and secondary schools in Sweden through data collection via each municipality.

The study is made easier to conduct in Sweden, which has a very strict policy on governmental responses to questions and requests for public documents: it is expected that all questions are responded to, and requested public documents must be provided.

The survey consists of 12 questions and 4 requests for public documents. The same questions and requests for public documents are used for both primary and secondary schools, and specifically concern the following aspects of students' IT usage:

- Software and IT equipment procured for and provided to the students.
- Evaluations of the use of adopted software and IT equipment.
- Software and document formats that students are required to have access to and regularly use to read, write and edit documents.
- Web-based systems that require registration of user accounts that students are required to have access to the school.
- Policies regarding installation, use, and maintenance of software.
- Agreements and regulations for student use of software and IT equipment.

For reasons of clarity (both for researchers and respondents) concerning interpretation of questions, requests, and responses, each question was duplicated in two versions (with an a-version for primary and a b-version for secondary schools). The only difference between the two versions was that the word "primary school" (in the a-version) was replaced by "secondary school" (in the b-version). Another reason for making the two versions explicit was that it was known in advance that different public sector schools and different municipalities are organised and operate in different ways. Hence, a response to the survey could potentially involve several persons and units in the organisation. This design allows for respondents covering both primary and secondary schools to just indicate "same" when responding for the b-version of each question. At time for the survey design, we had informal dialogues with practitioners in the domain in order to scrutinise our design and planned actions for data collection.

In this paper, we present initial results concerning the third and sixth aspect (marked bold above) for primary schools. When the data collection was initiated (January 2012), Sweden had 9.5 million citizens (in its 290 municipalities) of which 889000 were students in one of the 4616 public sector primary schools. It should be noted that a few (totally 3) municipalities have only one primary school (with totally less than 1000 students), whereas there are also (totally 2) municipalities with more than 100 primary schools (with totally more than 170000 students). Most (totally 281) municipalities have less than 10000 students and as the majority of all municipalities (totally 153) have less than 1500 we plan to account for differences in demographics and organisational structures in forthcoming phases of this research. For example, it is known that decision making and work practices impacting on IT usage in public schools differ between municipalities and schools. Therefore, forthcoming data collection will be directed to respondents in individual schools and other stakeholders who also have an impact on current practice. However, for our selection of the survey results reported on in this paper, such analysis and triangulation is not necessary.

For data collection, we sent an email containing the survey in plain text to each municipality (290 in all), with follow-up reminders sent over a seven month period. The text in the email was supplemented with two attachments (one ODF and one PDF/A-1b file) containing the survey. The survey clarifies, for reasons of privacy, that respondents can reply via email or by sending a letter containing printed documents.

The study resulted in both quantitative and qualitative data. Quantitative data was analysed to gauge the overall position with respect to informed decision making about students' IT usage in public sector schools. The text of responses, together with that of supplied documents, was analysed qualitatively, to give some insight into the real state of practice.

IV. RESPONSIVENESS TO THE QUESTIONNAIRE

The request email was sent to the registered address of each municipality. A municipality is required to respond promptly (at least with an acknowledgement), usually interpreted to mean within 24 hours. If no response was received within four working weeks, then a reminder was sent. This continued with, for each reminder, increased emphasis. It should be noted that the email included requests for public documents that they are required by law to respond to.

After the fourth reminder the email also included a clear request for an acknowledgement of receipt of the email, and after more than seven months of elapsed time since the initial request (and in one case after thirteen reminders) all municipalities had acknowledged receipt of the email. Initially, some municipalities seem to have ignored the survey despite the fact that it contains a request for public documents, whereas yet others explicitly declined to respond. Several provided partial responses, which are probed further. On average, it took 76 days and 2.7 reminders since the initial request before a municipality acknowledged receipt of the email, and even longer before receiving a survey response (at time of writing more than 1400 reminders have been sent concerning the questions in the survey and more than 1500 reminders concerning public documents). Many of these reminders contain clarifications and explanations, and a number of telephone conversations have also been used for clarifications.

Some municipalities explicitly declined to respond and others provided partial responses, which were probed further. Some delays were evidently caused by confusion over who should respond, no individual feeling able to respond to all requests. This meant that the email was circulated within and between organisations (as there are also different types of collaborations between schools and municipalities). In many cases this resulted in partial answers being given from different parts of an organisation and from the data collection process it is evident that several individuals were involved. Many respondents expressed reluctance to provide responses and all requested documents, and in some cases even some frustration.

The initial request was responded to by 10% of the respondents. A reminder elicited further responses, resulting in a 19% response rate and after a second reminder, 27% had responded . At time of writing, the response rate for the survey is 57%, but as several respondents have promised to respond later (and with further reminders) we expect the response rate to grow as the data collection continues. On average, it took 123 days and 4.9 reminders since the initial request before receiving these responses.

V. OBSERVATIONS FROM THE ANALYSIS

We present our analysis of survey responses related to the (two) specific questions and request for public documents:

- Which document formats (and versions of these) are students in primary schools in your municipality expected to manage in order to be able to read, write and edit documents (as well as to be able to exchange these documents electronically with teachers and other students) to be able to engage in school work?
- Which software (and versions of these) are students in primary schools in your municipality expected to have access to and regularly use in order to be able to read, write and edit documents (i.e. essays, instructions and other texts that students should prepare and communicate with teachers and other students) to be able to engage in school work?
- We kindly ask you to send us the documents (i.e. agreements, regulations, instructions and other documents) governing students' loan and use of IT equipment in primary schools in your municipality. We also kindly ask you to send us the documents which govern support, service and administration of software on this computer equipment.

All citations from survey responses and text from requested documents stem from our translation.

A. On use of document formats for writing essays

As writing essays, reports and other texts is one of the most common activities in primary schools, the survey investigates what a school expects from its students concerning use of specific document formats. The question specifically addresses expectations concerning use of specific document formats for management of documents, and in particular formats which provide the ability to read, write, edit, and exchange (with teachers and other students) documents.

From analysis of survey responses related to what schools expect from their students concerning use of specific document formats six broad categories emerged that could be meaningfully interpreted. These six categories represented 94% of all responses concerning what a school expects from its students and below we comment on our analysis of these. For the remaining 6%, it was not possible to give a meaningful interpretation due to lack of information in each response.

We make a number of observations from our analysis of responses in the identified six categories.

The first category (39%) includes responses for which it is evident that respondents understand what a document format actually is. For most of the responses in this category commonly used document formats are identified, see Table 1 for an overview of the most common formats. However, there were also some respondents which included file formats primarily aimed at other types of files (in addition to document formats) in their response. File formats primarily aimed at other types of files mentioned in responses include file formats for images (e.g. bmp, jpg, png and gif), video/multimedia (e.g. mpeg4, wmv, avi), and audio (e.g. wav). Several responses include expectations for use of several document formats.

TABLE 1: EXPECTATIONS CONCERNING DOCUMENT FORMATS FOR RESPONDENTS IN THE FIRST CATEGORY

Expected document formats	Percentage of respondents
doc	89
pdf	49
docx	44
odt	23
pages	5

From the second category of responses (29%), it is clear that many of those responding do not understand the concept of document format. Most respondents in this category mention software applications which schools expect students to use for writing essays and other documents. Responses include: "MS Office", "Word", "Office", "Open Office", "iWork", "Software which is compatible with MS Office", "Office Pro Plus 2003-2010", "MS Office 2010", "Microsoft Office 2007", "Word 2003", "Office 2003". There are also some responses in this category which included other types of software, file formats (not primarily aimed at editing text), and platforms, such as: "Fronter", "outlook.com", "word and pdf", and "Word for XP". A few responses in this category were more elaborated. For example, one respondent seems to equate "Word" with a document format: "In general it is word and PDF that we expect students to be able to read" and another responded with a policy for its municipality concerning document formats as follows: "The recommended document format in our municipality is Office 2007". As public primary schools are governed by municipalities, this policy (implicitly) also applies for all primary schools in this municipality. Others seem to be more aware of their unfamiliarity with the concept of document format. For example, as stated by one respondent: "I do not understand this fully. Primary schools and most schools use office software. I do not know what the student understands, nor how they have learnt the software. The educators in X-municipality may register for PIM but there is no explicit requirement for the level they are expected to achieve. Today this is up to each headmaster to decide."

The third category (18%) contains responses which refer to specific software with an explicit account for associated format without being specific about which document format they expect students to use. Hence, for these respondents it is clear that consideration of which software the school should expect students to use precedes any decisions on document formats. In essence, any expectation concerning use of document format is a consequence of their selection of which software they expect their students to use. Several responses in this category were vague and implicitly referred to formats provided by a specific vendor or product. For example, responses in this category include: "Microsoft's", "The formats in Office 2007", "The document formats which are supported by Apple", "The formats supported in Open Office", and "All formats which can be generated by our software". In other responses, the priority on software over document format was made even more explicit through inclusion of references to other parts of the survey where their response listed specific software, as illustrated by this example: "The document formats supported by the software [reference to response on another question]".

The fourth category (6%) includes a number of responses which made explicit that the school does not expect students to be able to use specific document formats. Several responses clarified that it does not matter, as illustrated by these responses: "Nothing is expected", "There are no documented guidelines or requirements", and "We currently do not have any such requirements". Some responses were more elaborated and the responses show some awareness of the challenges associated with different versions of document formats and different versions of software for those formats: "So far it has sometimes been difficult for primary school students and teachers because there are several versions of word processors and suppliers. The primary school currently strives for the iPad and we do not yet know what this will lead to".

Some respondents did not explicitly respond to the specific question concerning document formats, but it was still possible to identify expectations concerning use of document formats. This comprises the fifth category (6%) of responses. From analysis of responses to other questions in the survey (most notably those related to expectations concerning use of software) we included into this category responses which were explicit about expectations concerning software use. Hence, responses in this category (implicitly) clarified expectations and the responses were similar to those responses that were categorised into the third category (which explicitly expressed expectation regarding document formats).

The remaining responses were categorised into the sixth category (1%) and included a few responses in which respondents explicitly express uncertainty. Hence, these responses indicate a self-awareness of a lack of knowledge. As it was possible to give a meaningful interpretation for these responses (essentially awareness of lack of knowledge), we considered these to be somewhat different from those responses which gave no indication of the situation (that are also not included in any of the six categories).

From these survey responses, it is apparent that there is confusion concerning what a document format actually is and how choice of such formats may affect users. This includes awareness of the potential impact on students when schools express, explicit or implicit, expectations concerning such formats. In particular, there is considerable confusion amongst respondents concerning the difference between a document format and software systems aimed for reading, writing, and editing of documents.

B. On use of software applications for writing essays

Related to the issue of document formats, the survey also investigates what a school expects from its students concerning use of specific software for writing and managing documents. The question specifically addresses expectations from the school concerning use of specific software which students are expected to use for reading, writing, and editing text in documents when writing essays and other types of texts.

From analysis of survey responses it is clear that a majority of schools expect their students to use specific software applications (see Table 2 for an overview). Some respondents included details concerning which specific version of the software they expect their students to use, whereas others provided no such information. A number of responses include expectations for use of several software applications.

TABLE 2: EXPECTATIONS CONCERNING USE OF SOFTWARE APPLICATIONS FOR WRITING ESSAYS AND OTHER DOCUMENTS

Expected software applications	Percentage of respondents
Microsoft Office	75
OpenOffice	17
LibreOffice	7
iWork	2
Google docs	2
Others (responses included MS Live, Works etc).	2
Apple	1

In Table 2 we do not distinguish between responses that distinguish between "Microsoft Word" and "Microsoft Office" (with or without specific version number), all such responses are summarised into one row. Amongst respondents who included expectations concerning specific version, we note that Microsoft 2010, 2007, and 2003 dominate. However, responses that included version also mentioned 97, 2000, and 2002. For "OpenOffice", most respondents did not mention a specific version, but amongst those that did versions mentioned ranged from "OpenOffice 2.0" to "OpenOffice 3.3". For "LibreOffice", only one response mentioned a specific version (3.4.4).

To gain some additional insights concerning the relationship between expectations for document formats and software we specifically analysed the second category in sub-section 5.1 (i.e. the respondents that do not seem to understand the concept of document format) and investigated their expectations for software. From this, we find that 91% of those that do not seem to understand what a document format is expect students to use a proprietary licensed software (e.g. Microsoft Office and iWork), whereas the remaining 9% expect their students to use a software which is licensed under an Open Source software license (e.g. OpenOffice and LibreOffice) that can be obtained at no cost.

To further analyse the relationship between expectations for document formats and software we also analysed the first category in sub-section 5.1 (i.e. respondents that seem to understand the concept of document format) and investigated their expectation for software. From this, we find that only 3% expect their students to use document formats for which there is software applications provided as Open Source software.

C. On the agreements for use of IT equipment

To gain insights concerning agreements, regulations, and other instructions for students' use of IT in an educational context, the survey contains a request for public documents governing students' access to, and use of, IT equipment in primary schools. This request concerned documents which govern support, service, and administration of software on the computer equipment provided to students in primary schools. Some of these documents must be signed by the student and parents before the school provides access to the software, equipment, and network. From our analysis of agreements, regulations, rules, contracts, and other instructions we make a number of observation concerning underlying assumptions related to learning, innovation and educational lock-in.

Although almost all schools use a proprietary platform (in most cases a Windows platform) there are a few that use Linux. In addition to use of OpenOffice and LibreOffice (see Table 2), many schools also use at least some Open Source software (e.g. Firefox, VLC, Audacity, Blender, GIMP, etc.). Besides desktop PCs used in almost all schools, many schools also provide laptops to their students with preinstalled software motivated by a desire for improved education. Hence, in many schools at least some Open Source software will be preinstalled on equipment (PCs, laptops etc.) that is provided to students for use in school and for the case of laptops also at home.

Through analysis of requested documents a number of statements that seem perfectly fine with respect to innovation and Open Source software were identified. For example, concerning licenses one case states: "If the student installs software beyond what has been preinstalled, the student is required to obtain valid and legal licenses for the programs", and another: "In cases where software installations are made on your computer, it is the student's responsibility to ensure that valid licenses are available."

Similarly, the issue of copyright is clarified as follows: "Copying, downloading or distribution of copyrighted or otherwise protected material is permitted only if the right holder permits", and in another it is also made explicit that copyright also applies to software: "When something is 'copyrighted' you may just copy or disseminate it if the owner (holder) allows it. This also applies to software."

On the contrary, schools also use a number of statements which may inhibit innovation and contribute to lock-in. For example, under this regulation students are dependent on the IT department and students are not allowed to experiment with new software: "Only applications that the municipality's IT department and the school's system administrators provide are allowed for use on school computers." Similarly, in another case it is necessary for the student to get permission from the teacher before (installing or uninstalling) software: "It is not allowed to install anything on your computer without the teacher's permission. It is not allowed to uninstall software which is part of the computer's preinstalled software". In some cases, regulations make explicit that it is not allowed for other people to use the software, as clarified in this statement: "The legal guardian and his or her child is not entitled to install software or otherwise interfere with the computer."

Some regulations allow students to install software, but not to change the operating system as illustrated by this statement: "It is not allowed to install any other operating system than the one provided by the school."

In regulations used by schools that provide Open Source software on their computers, we find a number of misconceptions and restrictions concerning the ability for students to use, copy and redistribute the software. For example, one regulation restricts use of the software for sharing files: "File sharing of copyrighted materials is always prohibited", and another restricts distribution of software: "It is forbidden to copy the software which has been installed on your computer and install it on other computers (e.g. at home) unless the school has given permission for this." Another, perhaps even more interesting statement (given that an Open Source software license is a copyright license): "The student is responsible for that the computer is not used in a manner that violates any law, for example by downloading copyrighted material." Some schools use rather strong statements in order to inhibit copying and redistribution of the software they provided their students: "It is not allowed to copy software to or from school computers", and another case use the following statement: "It is forbidden by law to copy the software and trespassers will be prosecuted." Further, other statements constrain use (to non-commercial purposes), something which may be troublesome for school initiatives aimed at stimulating students to become young entrepreneurs during their studies: "It is not allowed to use the computer for commercial purposes, i.e. for activities which involve money and which are intended to produce income."

VI. Discussion and Conclusion

In a public speech in the Swedish context, the Swedish minister responsible for IT stated [12] (*our translation*):

"The objective of the Digital Agenda for Sweden is that Sweden will be the best in the world at using digitization opportunities. It is a goal that not only means that we should follow the trend, but we really should be at the forefront of it."

With this ambition in mind, it seems clear from the results of the survey that current practice is far from this ambition. To achieve this, the Swedish schools face significant challenges concerning IT education and usage.

Concerning use of document formats and software applications, survey results show that many schools expect that their students use document formats that are based on a technical specification which "is not complete" and "include references to proprietary technology and brand names of specific products" [8]. This, in light of survey results, imply that many students are expected to use proprietary software provided from a single vendor. Such expectations from schools are certainly not in line with the regulations from [21] concerning the requirement that "education shall be free of charge" for students in Swedish public schools, and also not in line with goals for using Open Standards as a basis for IT in the Swedish public sector in order to promote innovation.

Further, results show that current practice promotes use of software based on proprietary technologies, closed document formats, and a closed mindset for IT usage amongst students, as illustrated and characterised by a number of statements from regulations and contracts that students need to sign. From an innovation perspective, a more sustainable strategy would be to utilise solutions based on Open Standards for which there exist Open Source software implementations.

In the short term, it appears that an effective recommendation for schools based on the results would be to always undertake evaluations of document formats prior to decisions on software applications, and in so doing always consider interoperability and lock-in scenarios.

To conclude, results from the study suggest that there is significant scope for improvements in the Swedish formal education concerning IT usage. In particular, there are many misconceptions and significant unawareness amongst respondents. Many schools seem unaware of the potential with Open Standards and Open Source software as enablers for innovative use of IT that does not discriminate any student.

References

[1] J. Åsblom, "Halva priset för skoldator med Linux," ComptuerSweden, 26 Jan. 2012, www.idg.se/2.1085/1.428716/halva-priset-for-skoldator-med-linux

[2] G.B. Bird, "The Business Benefit of Standards," StandardView, Vol. 6(2), 76-80, 1998.

[3] DAE, "A Digital Agenda for Europe," COM(2010) 245 final/2 .

[4] EC, "Digital Agenda: Annual scoreboard confirms need for structural economic reform across Europe and surplus of ICT jobs; big trend towards mobile services and technology," European Commission, IP/12/614, Press Release, Brussels, 18 Jun. 2012.

[5] T.M. Egyedi, "An Implementation Perspective on Sources of Incompatibility and Standards' Dynamics," In Egyedi, T.M. and Blind, K. (Eds.) The Dynamics Of Standards, Edward Elgar Publishing, ISBN: 9781847204868, pp. 28-43, 2008.

[6] EU, "European Interoperability Framework for pan-European eGovernment Services, European Commission," Version 1.0 2004, http://ec.europa.eu/idabc/servlets/ Doca2cd.pdf?id=19528.

[7] EU, "From an IT policy for society to a policy for the information society, European Commission," 30 Jun., 2005, www.epractice.eu/files/media/media_208.pdf

[8] "Guidelines for Public Procurement of ICT Goods and Services: SMART 2011/0044, D2 - Overview of Procurement Practices," Final Report, Europe Economics, London, 1 Mar. 2012, cordis.europa.eu/fp7/ict/ssai/docs/study44-d2-finalreport.pdf

[9] E. Fichtelius, "Absurd brist på datorer i de svenska klassrummen ," 2012-08-27, DN.se Debatt: http://www.dn.se/debatt/absurd-brist-pa-datorer-i-de-svenska-klassrummen

[10] R.A. Ghosh, "Open Standards and Interoperability Report: An Economic Basis for Open Standards, FLOSSPOLS," Deliverable D4, 12 Dec. 2005, flosspols.org/deliverables/FLOSSPOLS-D04-openstandards-v6.pdf

[11] L. Guijarro, "Interoperability frameworks and enterprise architectures in e-government initiatives in Europe and the United States," Government Information Quarterly, Vol. 24(1), 89-101, 2007.

[12] A.-K. Hatt, "Från Lahore till Ale - It i elevernas tjänst, Public Speech at: 'It i skola och utbildning'," Nordiska skolledarkongressen, Gothenburg, 29 Mar., www.regeringen.se/sb/d/13698/a/189703 , 2012.

[13] Kroes, N. (2008). "Being Open About Standards." Brussels, June 10, SPEECH/08/317, European Commissioner for Competition Policy.

[14] B. Lundell, "e-Governance in public sector ICT procurement: what is shaping practice in Sweden?," European Journal of ePractice, Vol. 12(6), www.epractice.eu/en/document/5290101, 2011.

[15] B. Lundell, "Why do we need Open Standards?," In Orviska, M. and Jakobs, K. (Eds.) Proceedings 17th EURAS Annual Standardisation Conference 'Standards and Innovation', The EURAS Board Series, Aachen, ISBN: 978-3-86130-337-4, pp. 227-240, 2012.

[16] "Rundabordssamtal om it i skola och undervisning, Närings-departementet," 18 Feb. 2011, www.regeringen.se/sb/d/14390/a/161358

[17] M. Odell, "Mats Odell (Swedish minister), European Public Sector Award, Maastricht, 5 Nov. 2009 .

[18] "IT en rättighet för elever, Sveriges Kommuner och Landsting, Stockholm, 2011, www.skl.se/press/debattartiklar/debattartiklar-2011/it-en-rattighet-for-elever

[19] T.S. Simcoe, "Open Standards and intellectual property rights." In Chesbrough, H., Vanhaverbeke, W. and West, J. (Eds.) Open Innovation researching a new paradigm, Oxford University Press, Oxford, 2006..

[20] "Redovisning av uppdrag om uppföljning av IT-användning och IT-kompetens i förskola, skola och vuxenutbildning," Skolverket, Stockholm, Dnr 75-2007:3775 , 2010-04-09. 2010

[21] "Avgifter i skolan," Informationsblad, Skolinspektionen," 7 Dec. 2011, www.skolinspektionen.se/Documents/vagledning/infoblad-avgifter.pdf .

[22] "Strategi för myndigheternas arbete med e-förvaltning," Statens Offentliga Utredningar: SOU 2009:86, e-Delegationen, Finansdepartementet, Regeringskansliet, Stockholm, 19 Oct. 2009, www.sweden.gov.se/content/1/c6/13/38/13/1dc00905.pdf

Unsettling Users

Openness and the Rise of Inverse Infrastructures

Tineke M. Egyedi* and Wim Vree
ICT/TPM
Delft University of Technology
Delft, the Netherlands
*corresponding author T.M.Egyedi@tudelft.nl

Abstract—The rise of inverse infrastructures [1], i.e., user-driven, self-organizing emergent infrastructures, necessitates a paradigm shift in current thinking about infrastructures [2]. For such bottom-up developed infrastructures, open standards – e.g., standardized protocols, components and data in IT - are particularly important. This paper argues that they lower the threshold for inverse community innovation because they make user investments affordable, facilitate interoperability and ease the development of complementarities. Open standards thus catalyze user-driven developments that challenge dominant infrastructure practices and policies.

Index Terms—Open standards, self-organization, bottom-up emergent infrastructures, user innovation.

I. INTRODUCTION

Infrastructures are the backbones of networked societies and are overall viewed as a precondition for societal development and economic growth [3]. According to the current infrastructure paradigm, they are Large Technical Systems (LTSs) in the Hughesian sense [4, 5], designed top-down and operated centrally. The rational for a top-down and centralized approach is that this is the most efficient and least expensive way to manage the scale and complexity of infrastructure services (i.e., least transaction costs). Accordingly, government authorities and/or the commercial companies that assume responsibility for running infrastructure services such as water supply and sanitation, electricity and waste handling, play a key role in the current service provision. During the past decades their central role, responsibilities and interests have been institutionalized in regulation, contracts and standards.

However, increasingly infrastructures are emerging that are not run or owned by governments or large businesses. They are not governed centrally or controlled top-down by government or industry. Instead, they are developed by citizens or small businesses and yet manage to mushroom into local, regional and even global infrastructures. Examples are networks of privately-owned solar energy systems, citywide Wi-Fi networks and ham radio communication. These user-driven, self-organizing infrastructures, or *inverse infrastructures,* as Vree [1] coins them, are primarily characterized by bottom-up development and decentralized control. "[D]rawing on the word *invert* – to turn upside down – these infrastructures are called *inverse* because they display general patterns of emergence and development that are opposite in nature from those of large-scale infrastructures familiar to us today." [2, p.3] They constitute a radical alternative to the model of LTSs.

In the field of Information and Communication Technologies (ICTs), on which we focus, their number is rising sharply. Apart from the Internet, which is itself an inverse infrastructure, one may think of the numerous possibilities for ad hoc networks [1], peer-to-peer networks for exchanging digital content (e.g. Napster and BitTorrent [6]) and social media facilitated networks [7] such as Myspace, Facebook and Hyves.

Below, we describe three inverse cases in more detail: UUCP (Unix to Unix Copy Program), the phenomenon of city-wide Wi-Fi networks [8,9] and Wikipedia [10]. We then more systematically discuss the key characteristics of the inverse approach and summarize recent insights [11]. We hope to contribute to scientific research by indicating causal links between these characteristics and open standards. As we argue in the discussion, open standards facilitate community innovation in crucial ways and thus contribute towards the emergence of inverse infrastructures.

II. EXAMPLES OF INVERSE INFRASTRUCTURES IN ICT

UUCP. One of the earliest examples of an inverse infrastructure that achieved worldwide use, was the connection of computers through UUCP [12]. The acronym refers to a small set of programs and protocols for transferring files between computers across a wide range of different media.

At the end of the seventies and the beginning of the eighties, university groups started connecting their computers using UUCP. The system became very successful. It lies at the origin of email as we know it today and of the Usenet discussion platform. From the latter many other inverse initiatives have since sprung. It was the platform where Tim Berners-Lee announced the World Wide Web, Linus Torvalds announced the Linux project, and Marc Andreesen announced the creation of the Mosaic browser [13].

UUCP supported cheap connections using modems with conventional telephone lines. Therefore, it was already accessible to small university groups with computers and telephone lines. UUCP offered a large gain in functionality for a small increase in costs. In 1983 the number of UUCP hosts amounted to 550; it nearly doubled to 940 in the next year [14].

The UUCP programs and protocols were developed as part of the UNIX system. Innovations were presented in papers at USENIX conference sessions [15]. No specific standardization body was needed because the acceptance of UNIX software and its distribution in academic circles resulted in sufficiently uniform and interoperable systems (i.e., de facto standardization process). This manner of standardizing, that is, distribution of free software including the source code, was to become seminal to many other Internet related developments.

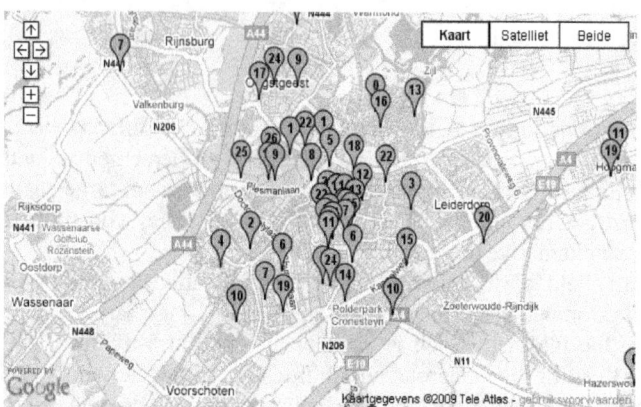

Figure 1: A node map of Wireless Leiden (April 2009)

Citywide Wi-Fi networks. A more recent example of an inverse infrastructure is the use of wireless Ethernet for citywide distribution of Internet. Wireless Ethernet (trademark Wi-Fi) [16], has become a very cheap standardized commodity that can be used to establish high-speed connections between nearby computers. With special software it is possible to organize computers in a web-like structure, which, using a technique called 'store and forward', can span city-wide areas. The advantage for participants in such a network is the low cost of Internet access that is achieved by sharing normal Internet connections (DSL) with other users. Since these connections are idle most of the time, sharing increases use efficiency from the perspective of the users. Of course, all communication within the boundaries of the Wi-Fi network is free.

Several citywide Wi-Fi networks exist. Some are commercial; some are sponsored by municipalities; and some are run by groups of volunteers. An example of the latter type is Wireless Leiden [8, 9, 17, 18]. This network evolved into an independent citywide infrastructure based on personal investments and efforts of both technically skilled and unskilled volunteers. Figure 1 shows a map with active nodes in the city center of Leiden [19].

Wikipedia. Wikipedia is a user-driven and self-organizing Internet-based encyclopedia. Its content is contributed and updated by volunteers who use the editing software of the wiki-platform to do so. Anyone can create new articles or edit existing ones, although in practice a relatively small number of people make a large number of edits [20]. Bots, i.e., small programs, are used to help volunteers support its maintenance (e.g. to detect unusual edits and repair malicious changes to Wikipedia articles) [10, p.117].

Trust-based self-organization in contributing content - without assigned editors – has allowed Wikipedia to mushroom [10].[1] This was aided by the self-reinforcing effect of participating in wikis in general (i.e., the more one contributes, the more others are also likely to contribute), network effects (i.e. the increase in the infrastructural value of the wiki with every new participant), and the reinforcing effect of its use on contributors [10]. The low threshold for using the encyclopedia (i.e., available to those with access to Internet) and has further facilitated its growth.

Wikipedia has become an important and - in many areas – a well-respected knowledge infrastructure. To indicate its size, the English-language Wikipedia contains 4,039,398 articles with an average of 19.71 revisions per article (August 29, 2012).

III. CHARACTERIZING INVERSE PHENOMENA

Inverse infrastructures largely develop unplanned, most often based on bottom-up user investments that have already been made. They are not 'designed' as GSM mobile telephony and high-speed railway infrastructures are, i.e., according to a predefined specification or blueprint. Given their developmental characteristics, their outcome is less predictable than that of designed infrastructures - although not without aim or direction.

Table I [11, Table 13.1] highlights who typically drives inverse infrastructure development; who makes initial investments; who owns the infrastructure; etc. It summarizes the characteristics of inverse infrastructure development and contrasts them with those typical of the design view on infrastructure LTSs dominant today. In this paper we discuss only the most prominent and prototypical characteristics. For an elaborate discussion of the Table see 'Inverse Infrastructures: Disrupting networks from below' [11].

User-driven. Describing inverse infrastructures as user-driven, we refer to the roles of those who initiate, maintain and/or coordinate their development. They are themselves the intended end-users, and may consist of professional users, individual consumers, households, institutions etc.

In general, social science research has increasingly shifted its focus from the production of technological artifacts to their consumption and use. While it formerly may have pictured users in a rather passive role, recent literature sheds a different light on the (potential) roles of users in technological change. It analyzes users individually and collectively as a source of unintended innovation (e.g., resulting from using existing products and services in unforeseen ways [22]) and of intended innovation (i.e., invited involvement in developing new products and services [23]).

---

[1] There are discussions on whether some form of editing should be introduced. (personal communication Chris Davis, June 2012)

TABLE I. CHARACTERISTICS OF INVERSE INFRASTRUCTURE DEVELOPMENT
[SOURCE: TABLE 13.1, 11]

Characteristic	Design Approach	Inverse Approach
Driven by	Providers (government, large companies)	Users (citizens, companies, government agencies, etc.)
Investments (technology, effort)	Providers (top-down)	Users (bottom-up, local)
Ownership infrastructure	Defined (providers)	Undefined or defined (incl. user, community and mixed ownership)
Governance	Centralized	Decentralized
Scale	Large	Small, may end up as large
Degree of homogeneity	Homogeneous	Heterogeneous, linked
Technology innovation	Classic, R&D-driven, by professionals	User innovation, innovation by experts
Coordination infrastructure development	Hierarchical (top-down), formal institutions	Self-organization (bottom-up), more informal institutions
Design focus on - where relevant	Content (blueprint of infrastructure)	Process (creating conditions for inverse development)
Outcome infrastructure development	Predefined	Less predictable, changing
Participants	Employed	Volunteers, self-employed or employed
Economy	Market-based	Reciprocity- & gift-based, non-financial self-interest, market-based

A second body of relevant research is that which throws light on why user-volunteers would be prepared to drive inverse developments. The term 'economy' [35] in Table I is used to capture the motives and rationales of volunteers to contribute. [11] addresses these motives in more detail. Here, we suffice by noting that studies of open source software communities [e.g., 24] are an important source of insight.

Self-organization. A characteristic feature of inverse infrastructures is self-organization among users. There are interesting parallels with self-organization in Complex Adaptive Systems (CAS) in, e.g., physics and biological sciences [25, 26]. According to CAS theory, self-organization as a mode of coordination in which control is dispersed and decentralized. *Mutatis mutandis*, this also applies to inverse phenomena [27]. In the example of city-wide Wi-Fi, individuals first make decentral attempts to optimize a local situation (e.g. installing Wi-Fi for home use). Subsequent interaction, combined with a small initial extra investment, leads to emergent system behavior – emergent as opposed to pre-determined – which lies at the roots of self-organization. The *infra*-structure qualities of inverse infrastructures emerge to a high degree spontaneously.
Some degree of coordination by means of self-organization is vital to the emergence and growth of inverse infrastructures. In the field of IT, standards are coordinative instruments *par excellence*. They are imperative for achieving interconnectivity, interoperability and data exchange. Standards may emerge (de facto) from interacting participants (e.g., UUCP and wiki-software); or they may have been developed elsewhere as open standards (e.g., IEEE 802.11 standards used in city-wide Wi-Fi networks).
In the example of the UUCP network, academic researchers self-organize who already cooperate in their scientific work. Note that in the case of city-wide Wi-Fi networks, participants must allow traffic from unknown users to pass through their own systems. The voluntary basis of self-organization makes this mode of coordination both special and vulnerable.

Decentralized infrastructure governance. Infrastructure governance refers to the means by which infrastructure development, operation and maintenance are coordinated. Finger et al. [28, p. 242] distinguish between centralized, decentralized and peer-to-peer coordination mechanisms, each of which can be differentiated by the level of decision-making involved. The first two are most significant for the study of inverse infrastructures[2]: "[a] centralized system uses a top-down approach, in which some centralized authority controls all major system elements or operations ... In a decentralized system, decision-making is distributed throughout numerous agents. System coordination is realized by certain institutional arrangements, but without any active planning or direct intervention" [28, p.242].

Clearly, what is regarded as central or decentral depends on one's perspective and the context under discussion. In this paper, we are foremost interested in the level of infrastructure *control* (i.e., next to coordination and decision making). On the European level, for example, national or regional control of electricity are considered decentral [29]; while from the point of view of inverse infrastructures, government control - whether local, regional, national, or supranational – will usually be viewed as centralized control. Here, we understand decentral control as being out of the hands of public administrators and large companies. (Note that we often use the terms *top-down* and *bottom-up* as twin concepts for centralized and decentralized governance, respectively.

IV.   DISCUSSION: OPENNESS

An inverse infrastructure in all its possible guises [11] represents a kind of community innovation [30]. To emerge and sustain, it requires openness technically, market-wise, institutionally and politically. Technically, for example, the inverse development of infrastructure applications is facilitated by stable and standardized software platforms (i.e., transparent unrestricted use, open source). Meanwhile, institutionally and

---

[2] They describe the third form: "Under the conditions of peer-to-peer coordination, self-selected agents mutually co-ordinate their activities based on bilateral agreements" [28, p.242]. Despite representing an extreme form of decentralization and the apparent applicability of peer-to-peer coordination to Internet and similar inverse infrastructures, the latter interactions typically go beyond bi-lateral agreements.

politically, current infrastructure policy and regulation, which have been tailored to the dominant top-down and centralized design approach, need to be reviewed on possible inhibitive effects for inverse developments [31].

TABLE II. REQUIRED OPENNESS FOR INVERSE INFRASTRUCTURE DEVELOPMENT

Characteristic	Inverse Approach	Openness
Driven by	Users (citizens, companies, government agencies, etc.)	Required: low threshold
Investments (technology, effort)	Users (bottom-up, local)	Required: low costs (standards-based competition), easy to use or develop further (standardized components, interoperability)
Ownership infrastructure	Undefined or defined (incl. user, community and mixed ownership)	Required: create regulation that can cope with no/more divers ownership
Governance	Decentralized	Required: review infra regulation on explicit/ implicit bias towards centralized governance
Scale	Small, may end up as large	Required: scalability technology
Degree of homogeneity	Heterogeneous, linked	Required: interoperability (standards)
Technology innovation	User innovation, innovation by lay and expert users	Required: recognition of interpretative flexibility and multi-directionality
Coordination infrastructure development	Self-organization (bottom-up), more informal institutions	Required: increase capacity of formal institutions to deal with informal set-ups & uncertain outcomes/ plans
Design focus on - where relevant	Process	Required: creating conditions for inverse development, abolish certain regulation?
Outcome infrastructure development	Less predictable, changing	Required: openness to unplanned, dynamic outcomes
Participants	Volunteers, self-employed or employed	Required: recognition of value and potential of diversity
Economy	Reciprocity- & gift-based, non-financial self-interest, market-based	Required: wider appreciation of what motivates and binds people

Table II summarizes the kind of openness that is needed to catalyze and/or allow emergent developments. Apart from requiring a reason to join inverse developments (e.g. significant added functionality, fun, social reasons), the ease and low costs of building an infrastructure are crucial to achieve sufficient initial infrastructure growth. Thereby open standards play a role in multiple respects. First of all, open[3] (compatibility[4]) standards help create a level playing field for IT producers. Open standards increase market transparency (i.e., facilitate product comparison, thus decreasing the chance of adverse selection) and are therefore more likely to foster competition (e.g., increased scale of production) and lead to lower prices. That is, standards-based products are likely to be cheaper and more widely available.

Second, apart from making user investments more affordable, standardized protocols, components and data facilitate compatibility. They ease the development of unplanned and unexpected complementarities. They lower the threshold for community innovation. Open standards can thus catalyze developments that are unsettling currently dominant infrastructure policies and practices.

Use existing (lower layer) infrastructures further reduces the cost of their development. For UUCP this was file transfer over telephone wires and for city-wide Wi-Fi it is sharing Internet connections through the air. Notably, the Internet has become a ubiquitous infrastructure upon which many other inverse infrastructures are built nowadays. Its role for these infrastructures is the same as that of the modem connections for the UUCP network in former days. Wikipedia the Bittorrent network for file sharing [32] are examples of Internet-based inverse infrastructures. (The Bittorrent network is a kind of distributed file storage where users can download multiple fragments of a file in parallel from different peer users that each have a copy of the file).

While lower layer standards are imperative for the emergence of large-scale inverse infrastructures, some form of additional standardization is required at the level of the inverse infrastructure service. Inverse infrastructures need specifications that support inverse developments (i.e., value-sensitive standards design). For example, the pioneers that established – peer-to-peer based - standards for the early Internet thereby facilitated the further development of TCP/IP based decentralized infrastructure services. In contrast, common mobile phone networks do not allow direct communication between end users. Why do nearby calls have to pass through the intermediary of an expensive operator? The communication range of a mobile phone can be several kilometres, and local calls could in principle be made directly without cost. This possibility has not been integrated in the standard specifications. Likewise, in the ISDN standard a centralized PTO-oriented mode of operating was embedded [34]. Whatever the reasons – paradigm-based, commercial, regulatory or other – those who develop the standard specification determine its content. Therefore, technologies and technical specifications that are crucial for inverse developments should be set by/ in close cooperation with user-developers.

V. CONCLUSION

Inverse infrastructures are unsettling the status quo. They are challenging current infrastructure practices and policies. We have argued in the previous that open standards are crucial for

---

[3] The European Interoperability Framework's (EIF) minimal requirements for an open standard, include the availability of a standard specification document for free or at a nominal charge, the availability of possible patents on a royalty-free basis, and no constraints on the re-use of the standard [33, p.9].

[4] Compatibility – here also equaled to interface or interoperability - standards – are most notable in ICT.

catalyzing their emergence. Open standards reduce the threshold (time, effort, finances) for participating in inverse developments by driving down the costs for extra initial investments; fostering interoperability thereby facilitating the contributions of volunteers (ease of access and use; ease of developing complementary products and services); and lower layers infrastructure standards highly ease (higher layer) inverse developments. That is, standards significantly facilitate community innovation and can therefore be viewed as a precondition for inverse infrastructure developments.

ACKNOWLEDGMENT

This paper builds on the Inverse Infrastructures project that was kindly funded by the Next Generation Infrastructures Foundation (http://www.nextgenerationinfrastructures.eu/), and which recently led to the publication of 'Inverse Infrastructures: Disrupting Networks from Below' [21].

REFERENCES

[1] W.G Vree, *Internet en Rijkswaterstaat: een ICT-infrastructuur langs water en wegen*. Inaugural speech, Delft: Delft University of Technology, 2003. Translated and reprinted in [21], pp. 267-290.
[2] Egyedi, T.M., Mehos, D.C, Vree, W.G. (2012), 'Introducing Inverse Infrastructures', in [21], pp. 1-16.
[3] ITU (2000), 'Section 7 of final report of ITU-D Focus Group 7: new technologies for rural applications', Telecommunication Development Bureau, ITU-D Study Groups, Document 2/179(Add.2)-E, 1 September 2000.
[4] T. P. Hughes, *Networks of Power: Electrification in Western Society* 1880-1930. Baltimore: Johns Hopkins University Press, 1983.
[5] E. van der Vleuten and A. Kaijser, "Prologue and introduction: Transnational networks and the shaping of contemporary Europe," in E. van der Vleuten and A. Kaijser, Eds., *Networking Europe: Transnational Infrastructures and the Shaping of Europe 1850-2000*. Science History Publications: Sagamore Beach, USA, 2006, pp. 1-22 .
[6] T.M. Egyedi, J.L.M. Vrancken and J. Ubacht, "Inverse infrastructures: Coordination in self-organizing systems," in:. *Proceedings of the 5th International Conference on Standardization and Innovation in Information Technology (SIIT 2007)*, P. Feng, D. Meeking & R. Hawkins, Eds.. Calgary,, Canada, 2007, pp. 23-35. Reprinted in [21], pp. 291-311.
[7] Boyd, D. and N. Ellison (2007), 'Social network sites: definition, history, and scholarship', Journal of Computer-Mediated Communication, 13 (1), article 11.
[8] Verhaegh,S., Van Oost, S. (2012), Who Cares? The Maintenance of a Wi-Fi Community Infrastructure; In [21], *pp. 141-160*.
[9] Lemstra, W, Hayes, V & Groenewegen, JPM (2010). *The innovation journey of Wi-Fi. The road to global success. Cambridge: Cambrdige University Press*
[10] Nikolic, I, Davis, C. (2012), Self-Organization in Wikis. In: [21], *pp. 103-124.*
[11] Egyedi T.M. (2012), Disruptive Inverse Infrastructures: Conclusions and Policy Recommendations,. In [21], *pp. 239-263.*
[12] M. Hauben, R. Hauben, and T. Truscott, *Netizens : On the History and Impact of Usenet and the Internet (Perspectives)*. Los Alamitos, CA.: Wiley-IEEE Computer Society, 1997.
[13] *Usenet* entry, wikipedia. Available: http://en.wikipedia.org/wiki/Usenet
[14] R. Kolstad and K. Summers-Horton, "Mapping the UUCP network," *Proceedings of 1984 USENIX UniForum Conference*, Washington, DC, 1984. Available: http://www.uucp.org/history/
[15] T. Cooklev, *Wireless Communications Standards: A Study of IEEE 802.11, 802.15 and 802.16*. New York: IEEE Press, 2004.
[16] R. van Drunen, D. van Gulik, J. Koolhaas, H. Schuurmans, and M. Vijn, "Building a wireless community network in the Netherlands, " *USENIX 2003 Annual Technical Conference*, June 2003, pp. 219-230. Available: http://www.usenix.org/publications/library/proceedings/usenix03/tech/freenix03/vandrunen.html
[17] R. D. J. Kramer, A. Lopez, and A. M. J. Koonen, "Municipal broadband access networks in the Netherlands - three successful cases, and how New Europe may benefit," *Proceedings of the 1st Int. Conf. on Access Networks*, Athens, Greece, 2006, ACM Int. Conf. Proc. Series; Vol. 267, Available: http://doi.acm.org/10.1145/1189355.1189367
[18] E. van Oost, S. Verhaegh and N. Oudshoorn, "From Innovation Community to Community Innovation: User-initiated Innovation in Wireless Leiden," *Science, Technology, and Human Values*, 34, 2009, pp. 182-205.
[19] Wireless Leiden . Available: Website: http://www.en.wirelessleiden.nl/
[20] Lieberman, M. and J. Lin (2009), 'You are where you edit: locating Wikipedia users through edit histories', in *Proceedings of Third International Conference on Weblogs and Social Media*, http://www.aaai.org/Library/ICWSM/ icwsm09contents.php.
[21] T.M Egyedi & D.C Mehos (Eds), *Inverse Infrastructures*: Disrupting networks from below. Cheltenham: Edward Elgar, 2012.
[22] N. Oudshoorn and T. Pinch, "User-technology relationships: Some recent developments, "in *The Handbook of Science and Technology Studies*, 3rd ed., E. Hackett, O. Amsterdamska, M. Lynch, and J. Wajcman, Eds., Cambridge: MIT Press and Society for the Social Studies of Science, 2008, pp. 541-565.
[23] Chesbrough, Henry (2003), *Open Innovation: The New Imperative for Creating and Profiting from Technology*, Boston: Harvard Business School Press.
[24] Raymond, Eric S. (1999), *The Cathedral and the Bazaar*, Sebastopol, CA: O'Reilly.
[25] M. Gell-Mann, *The Quark and the Jaguar: Adventures in the Simple and the Complex*. New York: Freeman & Co., 1994.
[26] J.H. Holland, *Hidden Order: How Adaptation Builds Complexity*. Reading, MA: Addison-Wesley, 1995.
[27] J. van den Berg, "Inverse infrastructures and their emergence at the edge of order and chaos: An analytic framework," in [21], 2012, *pp. 17-38*.
[28] M. Finger, J.Groenewegen, and R. Künneke, "The quest for coherence between institutions and technologies in infrastructures," *Journal of Network Industries*, 6 , 2005, No. 4, 227-259.
[29] V. Langedijk, *Electrifying Europe: The Power of Europe in the Construcction of Electricity Networks*. Amsterdam: Aksent, 2008.
[30] Van Oost, E., S. Verhaegh and N. Oudshoorn (2009), 'From innovation community to community innovation: user-initiated innovation in Wireless Leiden', *Science, Technology, & Human Values*, **34** (2), 182-205.
[31] R. Künneke, " The co-evolution between institutions and technologies in infrastructures: The case of inverse infrastructures" in [21], 2012, pp. 39-54.
[32] J. Pouwelse, P. Garbacki, D. Epema, H. Sips *The Bittorrent P2P File-Sharing System: Measurements and Analysis*, Lecture Notes in Computer Science, Volume 3640/2005, ISBN 978-3-540-29068-1, http://dx.doi.org/10.1007/11558989_19
[33] European_Commission_IDABC (2004). European Interoperability Framework for Pan-European eGovernment services, version 1.0.
[34] Mansell, R. and R. Hawkins (1992), 'Old roads and new signposts: trade policy objectives in telecommunication standards', in F. Klaver and P. Slaa (eds), *Telecommunication, New Signposts to Old Roads*, Amsterdam: IOS Press, pp. 45-54.
[35] Zeitlyn, D. (2003), 'Gift economies in the development of open source software: anthropological reflections', *Research Policy, 32*, 1287-1291.

Copyright, Interfaces, and a Possible Atlantic Divide

Simonetta Vezzoso
University of Trento
Trento, Italy
simonetta.vezzoso@unitn.it

Abstract— Recent copyright cases on both sides of the Atlantic focused on important interoperability issues. While the decision by the Court of Justice of the European Union in *SAS Institute, Inc v World Programming Ltd* assessed data formats under the EU Software Directive, the ruling by the Northern District of California Court in *Oracle America, Inc v Google Inc* dealt with application programming interfaces. The European decision is rightly celebrated as a further important step in the promotion of interoperability in the EU. This article argues that, despite appreciable signs of convergence across the Atlantic, the assessment of application programming interfaces under EU law could still turn out to be quite different, and arguably much less *pro*-interoperability, than under US law.

1. Introduction

In the field of intellectual property law, interoperability refers mainly to the ability of information technology products to communicate, i.e. to exchange signals and data. From a user's perspective, products, or systems, are considered to be interoperable if they can work together. Beyond IT markets, assuring the compatibility of products with those of other brands can also be essential in order to assure the satisfactory working of competition processes.

Interoperability (and compatibility) has obvious intrinsic value and, therefore, it is in the interest of society to support them. Seemingly, there are often private incentives at work that make undertakings spontaneously release the relevant interface information. For instance, it can be in the interest of a platform owner to share the rules of interconnection between her core technological building blocks and the surrounding ecology in order to promote the development of sets of complementary products and services and, by that, increase the overall attractiveness of the platform. From a business' perspective, decisions about the desired level of interoperability are both technology and market based, ultimately depending on the firm's expectations about its ability to create and capture economic value. In this respect, practices relating to interoperability can have positive or negative effects on the level of healthy competition, both *infra*- and *inter*platform.

The most significant *ex-ante* rules on interoperability in IT markets are presently located in the area of copyright law. Ideally, the latter should provide market participants with clear indications as to the ability to access and use interoperability information.

Unsurprisingly, perhaps, this approach delivers only partially satisfactory results. With regard in particular to Europe, the Software Directive has some indefinite language on the crucial issue of interoperability, and courts have been rather slow in delivering the necessary interpretative rulings. More than twenty years after the enactment of the EU Software Directive, the Court of Justice of the European Union ("CJEU") in *SAS Institute, Inc v World Programming Ltd* (C-406/10) (hereinafter *SAS v. WPL)*, articulated for the first time an explicit ban on copyright protection in what are some building blocks of software, such as programming language and data formats. Moreover, the decision denies copyright protection to the functional effects of software. On the whole, the recent CJEU's pronouncement provides those conducting the emulation of existing programs with some much less shaky legal ground covering their activities (Section 2, *infra*). The accrued legal certainty could have positive effects on competition in software markets. On the negative side, still unanswered under EU law are very important issues regarding interoperability, such as those decided in the US *Oracle America, Inc v Google Inc* (C 10-3561) (hereinafter *Oracle v Google*) (Sections 3 and 4, *infra*).

2. *SAS v WPL* and the EU Software Directive

Computer programs are protected as literary works under copyright law, within the meaning of the international Berne Convention for the Protection of Literary and Artistic works. Therefore, the written program code (both source and object code) is protected under copyright law, by analogy with other literary works such as the text of a novel or poem. Based on the legal doctrine known as the idea/expression dichotomy, it is well understood that the scope of copyright protection for computer programs is limited to the expression of the program. The main rationale behind the idea/expression dichotomy is that it is socially desirable to allow for the free use of the fundamental building blocks (the "ideas") of knowledge production in the area of copyright protection.

The idea/expression distinction proved a solid theme in support of the proposal of copyright protection for computer programs in the EU put forth in 1989.[1] Article 1(2) of the subsequently enacted EU Software Directive[2] states that

---
[1] See Proposal for a Council Directive on the legal protection of those computer programs, COM(88) 816 final, OJ 12.4.89, No C 91/4, at § 3.7, available at http://aei.pitt.edu/13138/1/COM_(88)_816_final.pdf.
[2] Council Directive 91/250/EEC of 14 May 1991 on the legal protection of computer programs, replaced by European Parliament and Council Directive

"[i]deas and principles which underlie any element of a computer program, including those which underlie its interfaces, are not protected by copyright." However, what exactly constitutes the "idea" of a literary work, excluded as such from copyright protection, stirs very lively debates, in Europe and elsewhere.

The question can be usefully framed in terms of the extent to which copyright infringement can consist in non literal copying of the work. The concept of non literal copying derives from traditional copyright law, and indicates that infringement in a work can take place even though there was little or nothing of the actual work that was used. Thus, for instance, the plot of a novel may be protected by copyright and infringed even when there is no evidence that literal copying (i.e. actual copying of the text) has occurred. With respect to the non literal copying of computer program, however, an extra layer of complexity is added because of the dual nature of computer programs, that is "textual works created specifically to bring about some set of behaviors"[3]. Thus, whereas a computer program *behaves*, more traditional works protected by copyright, such as books, manifestly do not, and a too broad interpretation of the "plot analogy" could inappropriately extend copyright protection to the functional aspects (the behaviour) of a computer program.

The recent *SAS v WPL* ruling by the CJEU touches upon a whole set of crucial legal issues concerning the object and scope of the copyright protection of computer programs in the EU, thus extending well beyond interoperability issues. World Programming Ltd ("WPL") had carefully studied very successful analytical software developed by the SAS Institute ("SAS"), which enabled users to write and run application programs to perform data processing and analysis tasks. Thereupon WPL created an alternative computer program (system/platform) allowing users to execute application programs already written in the SAS language, and ensuring that the same inputs would produce the same outputs. WPL's explicit goal was to enable SAS customers to run their own application programs written in the SAS language on WPL's alternative platform.

The preliminary reference from the English High Court[4] gave the CJEU the overdue opportunity to start clarifying, among other things, the scope of protection against non literal copying of computer programs. Importantly, in the *SAS* decision it was not established that the defendant in the national copyright infringement case, WPL, had access to object or source code and/or carried out any decompilation of the object code. WPL merely studied how the SAS program worked by performing "black box" analysis and reading the SAS manuals. WPL then wrote its own program to emulate the SAS program's functionality, i.e. the specific processing and analysis tasks performed by the program. The subject-matter "taken" by the defendant WPL, and which was at the basis of the allegation of copyright infringement, included the functionality of the SAS computer program, its language, and data formats.

In answering the questions posed by the national judge, the CJEU basically follows the opinion[5] previously delivered by its Advocate General ("AG") Yves Bot, but there are also a few differences worth emphasizing.

In his opinion, AG Bot first iterated the important role played by the internationally acknowledged idea/expression dichotomy in the area of copyright protection of computer programs. According to AG Bot, the reason underlying this core copyright principle would be that "the originality of a work, which gives access to legal protection, lies not in an idea, which may be freely used, but in its expression" (para. 44). It is perhaps necessary to remind at this point that the Software Directive deliberately left to the courts the task of ascertaining the boundaries of this central dichotomy within the EU, but this has unfortunately created broad areas of uncertainty and possibly missed more ambitious harmonisation objectives.

With regard to the scope of copyright protection for computer programs, AG Bot suggested that this is "conceivable only from the point at which the selection and compilation of those elements are indicative of the creativity and skill of the author and thus set his work apart from that of other authors" (para 48). Like a book author, the programmer "selects the steps to be taken and the way in which those steps are expressed gives the program its particular characteristics of speed, efficiency and even style" (para. 47).

As to the object of protection according to the Software Directive, AG Bot referred to Case C-393/09 *Bezpečnostní softwarová asociace – Svaz softwarové ochrany v Ministerstvo kultury*[6], decided in December 2010, in which the CJEU stated that protected is "the expression in any form of a computer program which permits reproduction of that program in different computer languages, such as the source code and the object code (…) from the moment when its reproduction would engender the reproduction of the computer program itself, thus enabling the computer to perform its function" (para. 49). The AG Bot therefore came to the conclusion that "the protection of a computer program is not confined to the literal elements of that program, that is to say, the source code and the object code, *but extends to any other element expressing the creativity of its author*" (para. 50 emphasis added).[7]

With respect to the functionalities of a computer program, AG Bot defined the latter as "the set of possibilities offered by a computer system, the actions specific to that program" (para. 52). He concluded that the functionalities "as such" cannot

---

[2] 2009/24/EC of 23 April 2009 (consolidated version, partial renumbering). The CJEU in *SAS v WPL* refers to the text of the 1991 Directive.

[3] Pamela Samuelson, Randall Davis, Mitchell D. Kapor, & J.H. Reichman, "A Manifesto on the Legal Protection of Computer Programs" (1994) , 94 COLUM. L. REV. 2308, 2320.

[4] *SAS Institute Inc v World Programming Ltd* [2010] EWHC 1829 (Ch).

[5] Opinion of AG Bot, delivered on 29 November 2011, Case C-406/10, *SAS Institute, Inc v World Programming Ltd*.

[6] [2010] ECR I-3971.

[7] See the 1989 Proposal (n.1), para. 1.1 ("a set of instructions the purpose of which is to cause an information processing device, a computer, to perform its functions").

form the object of copyright protection under Article 1(1) of the Software Directive (para. 53). According to AG Bot, the multitude of actions "dictated by a specific and limited purpose" (e.g. performing online hotel bookings), are similar to an idea, and therefore other computer programs should be able to offer the same functionalities (para. 54). Eligible for copyright protection are instead "the many means of achieving the expression of those functionalities", i.e. "the way in which the elements" composing a computer program "are arranged, like the style in which the computer program is written" (para. 55).

The CJEU squarely endorses the Advocate General's statement according to which to accept that the functionality of a computer program can be protected by copyright "would amount to making it possible to monopolise ideas, to the detriment of technological progress and industrial development" (para. 40; AG Bot para. 57). It should also be noticed that the language employed by the CJEU and AG Bot strongly resonates with previous US decisions stating that copyright protection of computer programs should not extend to the program's functionality because this would hamper scientific progress, ongoing innovation and competition in the marketplace.[8] This in turn mirrors the concern expressed by the already recalled TRIPS Agreement and WCT provisions that copyright protection for computer programs should not extend to "ideas, procedures, methods of operation, and mathematical concepts".[9] Moreover, the CJEU refers to the explanatory memorandum to the Proposal for a Software Directive[10], pointing out that by protecting "only the individual expression of the work", other authors would have had ample latitude "to create similar or even identical programs provided that they refrain from copying" (para. 41). Interestingly, the CJEU does not seem to conform to the exact, and arguably more restrictive, language employed by AG Bot, who, as we have seen above, referred to "functionalities as such."

Beyond SAS computer functionalities, the subject-matter "taken" by the defendant WPL included SAS programming language and data formats. Therefore, the CJEU had further to decide whether the programming language and the format of data files are protectable by copyright law under the Software Directive, i.e. whether they constitute a form of expression of the program.

With respect to "programming language and the format of data files used in a computer program in order to exploit certain of its functions", the Court concludes that they do not "constitute a form of expression of the program and therefore are not protected by copyright in computer programs according to the EU Software Directive" (para. 46). Referring once more to *Bezpečnostní softwarová asociace*, the Court does not exclude the possibility that "the SAS language and the format of SAS Institute's data files might be protected, as works, by copyright" under general copyright rules if "they are their author's own intellectual creation" (para. 45).

In his Opinion to the CJEU, AG Bot argued with regard specifically to SAS programming language, that this is "a functional element which allows instructions to be given to the computer (...) made up of words and phrases known to everyone and lacking originality." Thus, concludes the AG, "programming language must be regarded as comparable to the language by the author of a novel. It is therefore the means which permits expression to be given, not the expression itself" (para. 71).

The assessment of interfaces in the form of data formats put forth by the CJEU in *SAS* offers further and most needed clarification, based as it is on the legal interpretation of less than crystal clear language of the EU Software Directive.

To understand this, it should first be considered that interface specifications are concrete, in written form and normally forming part of the code. Second, despite often challenging constraints, there could still be some room for programmer's choices among functionally identical way of formulating the interface specifications, in that case satisfying the Software Directive's originality requirement. Third, the Directive does not state that copyright protection is unavailable to interfaces as such. Nevertheless, various recitals and articles would more or less explicitly promote interoperability.[11]

With respect specifically to data formats, the referring UK High Court asked whether it is an infringement for a program to be implemented in such a way that enables that same program to read and write data files that are in the format devised by another program. It is perhaps useful to recall at this point that WPL had reportedly obtained the interface information merely by studying how the SAS system operated. Specifically, WPL worked out enough of the data formats employed by the SAS system to be able to write a new source code that read and wrote data files written in that format, by that achieving interoperability with SAS users' computer programs (scripts).

As anticipated above, the CJEU denied copyright protection to data formats under the Software Directive. The Court in particular reminded that "WPL did not have access to the source code of SAS Institute's program and did not carry out any decompilation of the object code of that program" (para. 44), by that clearly differentiating its own assessment of the relevant facts from AG Bot's imprecise view that WPL had performed an act of decompilation (AG Bot, para. 83), and by that neutralising the very restrictive interpretation of the decompilation provision put forth by AG Bot, who pointed *inter alia* to the necessity for the licensee to demonstrate the "absolute necessity" of its actions.[12]

---

[8] Pamela Samuelson, "Why Copyright Law Excludes Systems and Processes from the Scope of Its Protection" (2007) *85 Texas Law Review*, 1921, 1934.

[9] TRIPs art. 9(2); WCT art. 2.

[10] *Supra* (n. 1).

[11] Pamela Samuelson, Thomas Vinje, And William Cornish, "Does Copyright Protection Under the EU Software Directive Extend to Program Behaviour, Languages and Interfaces?" (2011) 34 *European Intellectual Property Review*, 156, 163.

[12] Cfr. Sally Weston "Software Interfaces – Stuck in the Middle: The Relationship Between the Law and Software Interfaces in Regulating and Encouraging

However, both with regard to the SAS language and the format of SAS Institute's data files, the CJEU concluded that they might be protected, as works, by copyright under general copyright rules if they are their respective author's own intellectual creation (para. 45). While this last remark would seem to make the Court's holding on the issue of interfaces under EU law less clear-cut that some would have wished, it is nevertheless hard to dispute that the Court's explicit reference to the "general" copyright Directive[13] should not be read as authorizing the sweeping vacation of the fundamental copyright principle, enshrined in international copyright law, that ideas cannot be protected.

While the *SAS v WPL* decision should be welcomed[14], it still remains to be seen if the language chosen by the CJEU will make the *SAS* decision sufficiently operational, especially with respect to the idea/expression dichotomy as applied to computer programs, considering that this case is bound to be carefully deciphered by other courts and various stakeholders in the months and years to come.

Needless to say, of particular importance are the possible repercussions of the *SAS* decision on interoperability issues that were not expressly covered by this ruling, such as the copyright protection of application programming interfaces ("APIs"). The remaining parts of this article briefly consider how a District Court on the other side of the Atlantic recently decided the question of the copyrightability of APIs. This article concludes that it is far from inevitable that a court on this side would come to a similar conclusion under EU law.

3. ORACLE V GOOGLE AND THE COPYRIGHT PROTECTION OF APIS

In 2010, shortly after having acquired Sun Microsystems, Inc., Oracle sued Google for infringement of Java-related copyrights and patents. The *Oracle v Google* case turned out to be a complex dispute, finally decided by the San Francisco Judge William Alsup on June 20, 2012, that is only a few weeks after the CJEU issued the SAS ruling considered in the previous Section.[15]

Most interesting for our purposes, Judge Alsup had in particular to decide whether the structure, sequence and organization ("SSO") of application programming interfaces ("APIs") are protected under US copyright law. It should first be reminded that the phrase *structure, sequence and organization* does not appear in the US Copyright Act. Nevertheless, it has become a sort of metaphor for non literal copying of computer programs, whereas the more general issue under copyright law, as mentioned before, originally emerged with respect to traditional works such as books.

Thus, with regard specifically to the non literal copying of software, that phrase "SSO" captures the thought that the structure or order could, under specific circumstances, lie on the expression side of the idea/expression dichotomy. Specifically, in the case at issue it was alleged that Google's Android platform had copied the SSO of the overall code for 37 APIs packages of Oracle's Java platform. Interestingly enough, it was the first time that a decision by a US Court waded into the issue of the copyrightability of APIs. Judge Alsup came to the conclusion that Google had not infringed Oracle's Java-related rights, in particular because Oracle could not claim any copyright to the SSO of Java APIs.

Similarly to the SAS data formats, the APIs are interfaces that allow software programs communicate with each other. In particular, the Java APIs specify the behaviour of program modules, while the so called class library is the compiled object code implementing API specifications. By consulting the respective APIs, programmers can make use of specific program modules without having to know the details of the modules' inner workings. Communication between software programs is achieved by following the same set of specifications.

Java has currently 209 API "packages" for the Java Standard Edition, from the only 8 packages it had in 1996, when Java was first released. API design is a very complex task, involving difficult choices, and requiring significant expertise and time.[16] Java API "packages" are broken into "classes" and "methods", that is they are articulated in pre-written programs (classes) carrying out subroutines (methods). Whereas APIs change in time, the Executive Committee of the Java Community Process has approved only three changes of the Java language so far.

The Android platform for mobile devices was launched in 2007, most likely as a reaction to the threat that the emergence of smartphones posed to Google's core business model. The Android platform uses the Java programming language, the Dalvik virtual machine, and provides 168 own API packages, many of which have the same functions of Java APIs, but different design. However, Google replicated the SSO of 37 Java API packages, possibly those that "typical" Java programmers would expect to be callable by the same names used in Java and which were key to mobile devices. Specifically, Google used different code to implement the classes and methods of 37 Java API packages, but replicated their exact names and functions. In total, Google wrote – or acquired - to 97 percent new code, whereas the remaining 3

Interoperability," (2012) *International Review of Intellectual Property and Competition Law (IIC)*, 427, 442.

[13] Directive 2001/29/EC of the European Parliament and of the Council of 22 May 2001 on the harmonisation of certain aspects of copyright and related rights in the information society (OJ 2001 L 167, p. 10).

[14] Jochen Marly, "Der Schutzgegenstand des urheberrechtlichen Softwareschutzes," (2012) *GRUR*, 773, 778.

[15] Final Judgment. Throughout this article reference will be made to Judge Alsup's *Order re copyrightability of certain replicated elements of the Java application programming interface*, available at http://docs.justia.com/cases/federal/district-courts/california/candce/3:2010cv03561/231846/1202/0.pdf?ts=1338544292.

[16] For instance, the Oracle chief Java architect testified during the trial that it took him and his team of engineers two years to develop the java.nio. package.

percent consisted of replicated overall name organization and functionality.

As a result, applications written in the Java language can call the 37 sets of functionalities in Android by the same names as used in Java. Computer programs already written for the Java platform can run on Android to the extent that they call functionalities of those 37 sets. It follows that computer programs written to run on Java are to a certain extent able to run also on the Android platform. Conversely, programs written for the Android platform are not fully compatible with the Java platform. In this respect, the compelling concept "write once, run anywhere" does not hold true anymore for programs written in the Java language.

With regard to the exact nature of the Java SSO replicated by Google, to the extent that this turns out to be relevant to their copyright assessment, Judge Alsup drew a distinction between, first, the declaration or method header lines; second, the method and class names; third, the grouping pattern of methods (p. 5 ff.).

As to the first, the San Francisco District Judge concluded that "(u)nder the rules of Java, they *must be identical* to declare a method specifying the *same* functionality — even when the implementation is different" (p. 3, emphasis in the original). Put differently, since "every method and class is specified to carry out precise desired functions"; it follows that the header (non-implementing code) line of code "stating the specifications must be identical to carry out the given function" (p.5). Therefore, since there was only one way to express an idea or function, this under US merger doctrine must be free for everybody to use (p.35). According to that well-established doctrine, "courts will not protect a copyrighted work from infringement if the idea underlying the copyrighted work can be expressed in only one way, lest there be a monopoly on the underlying idea."[17]

With regard to the second, i.e. method and class names, and third, i.e. the way in which the methods are grouped, there is not the same "functionality constrain" as with the header lines. Nevertheless, Judge Alsup decided that there was no copyright infringement.

Specifically, with regard to method and class names, the legal argument presented by Judge Alsup was that "copyright protection never extends to names or short phrases as a matter of law" (p.2).

The assessment of the way in which methods are grouped turned out to be perhaps the most delicate aspect of the whole decision. In fact, Judge Alsup basically agreed with Oracle's assertion that in Android the methods could have been arranged in ways different from Java's groupings and yet offering the same functionality. However, according to the US District Judge, "while the overall scheme of file name organization resembles a taxonomy, it is *also* a command structure for a system or method of operation of the application programming interface" (p.37, emphasis in the original), "a long hierarchy of over six thousand commands to carry out pre-assigned functions" (p.38). The command structure is "a utilitarian and functional set of symbols, each to carry out a pre-assigned function". It therefore qualified as "system or method of operation" under Section 102(b) of the US Copyright Act, and could not be copyrighted, even if it original or even creative.

According to Judge Alsup, the interoperability argument would provide further support to the overall analysis of the Java grouping of methods under US copyright law just recalled, and in particular its character as a functional system or method of operation. The "fragmentation" among platforms lamented by Oracle during the trial, i.e. of the flawed interoperability between the Android and the Java platforms, was due to the fact that only Java-based applications using exclusively the replicated parts of the 37 API packages were Android-compatible. In case Java-based code needed a 38th package, it could not run on the Android platform. Therefore, insofar as the command structure for the 37 Java API packages was replicated in Android, third-party source code relying on those packages could run on the Android platform, by that achieving a certain level of interoperability/compatibility. In fact, those APIs whose organization differed from Java APIs would not have been interoperable, "for the name structure itself dictates the precise form of command to call up any given method" (p.12).

According to US case law, interface procedures that needed to be replicated in order to achieve interoperability were "*functional* requirements for compatibility" (emphasis mine), as such not copyrightable under Section 102(b). Finally, full interoperability was not relevant to the Section 102(b) analysis (p.39)

4. Conclusion: legal assessment of APIs under the EU Software Directive?

Inevitably, even a cursory look across the Atlantic raises the question how a similar or identical case would have been decided by a national judge applying EU law. In the following it will be explained that, despite the influential CJEU decisions in *SAS* and *Bezpečnostní softwarová asociace*, there is still no obvious answer to this important issue concerning interoperability under EU law. But it can be reasonably expected that, given the Software Directive's clear intent to foster interoperability, courts treat infringement claims involving APIs with the necessary care.

Undoubtedly, the part of the *SAS* decision concerning computer program's functionalities illustrates an interesting convergence between the software copyright regimes across the North Atlantic, also consistent with international treaty obligations. In fact, both the Agreement on Trade-Related Aspects of Intellectual Property Rights and the World Copyright Treaty state that copyright protection for computer programs should not extend to ideas, procedures, methods of operation, or mathematical concepts. As reminded both by the CJEU in *SAS* and by Judge Aslup in *Oracle v. Google*, ideas

---

[17] *Satava v. Lowry*, 323 F.3d 805, 812 n.5 (9th Cir. 2003).

and functions cannot be monopolized by way of copyright protection.

Of course, the idea/expression dichotomy and the banning of functionalities from copyright protection apply to methods in APIs as well. Thus, as explained in nicely plain words by the US District Court judge, everybody is free to write her own code to carry out a function (i.e. comparing two numbers and returning the greater) "so long as the implementing code in the method body is different from the copyrighted implementation" (p.34). Especially after the *SAS* decision, there should be little doubt that, under EU law, a Court applying the crucial idea/expression distinction to APIs is bound to come to roughly the same conclusion as the US judge. Moreover, also AG Bot drew a clear distinction between data files as "blank forms which are to be filled with the customer's data by the SAS System and which contain specific locations in which particular information must be written in order for the system to be read and write the file correctly" (para. 79) and the "the elements which create, write and read the format of said SAS data files" which are "expressed in source code in the program", and concluded that SAS source code implementing the data format could be copyrightable (paras. 81-82). Similarly, one could argue that the idea represented by the API is not copyrightable, whereas the source code implementing the API in principle is protected.

But, as seen above, Google went further than that, and its actions raised in particular the question whether the SSO of the API could be copyrightable.

First, Google replicated the *method specification* as set forth in the declaration. However, Judge Aslup ascertained that under the Java rules, the declaration must be precise; otherwise it would carry out some other function. Therefore, to this "part" of the broader API issue, the US judge decided to apply the merger doctrine, which bars the claiming of copyright ownership in an expression if there is only one way to formulate something.

Under EU law, it is not sure whether the conclusion on this specific point would be the same. For once, the status of the merger doctrine under EU law is considered to be uncertain.[18] It should be reminded, however, that the already mentioned Software Directive's original proposal[19] contained a rather explicit reference to that doctrine where it said that "(i)f similarities in the code which implements the ideas, rules or principles occur as between inter-operative programs, due to the inevitability of certain forms of expression, where the constraints of the interface are such that in the circumstances no different implementation is possible, then no copyright infringement will normally occur, because in these circumstances it is generally said that idea and expression have merged." Moreover, the CJEU in *Bezpečnostní softwarová asociace*, while discussing the issue of "additional" protection for graphical user interfaces under general copyright law, held that "where the expression of those components [which form part of the graphic user interface, *SV*] is dictated by their technical function, the criterion of originality is not met, since the different methods of implementing an idea are so limited that the idea and the expression become indissociable" (para. 49). The Court's explanation, however, did not refer to the idea/expression dichotomy, but to the lack of originality, when in the following paragraph it explained that "(I)n such a situation, the components of a graphic user interface do not permit the author to express his creativity in an original manner and achieve a result which is an intellectual creation of that author" (para. 50).[20]

Going back to the US decision, Judge Aslup further held that the copying of the *method and class names* cannot give rise to copyright liability, for under US law, names and short phrases cannot be copyrighted in the first place. Again, under EU law the conclusion on this aspect of the broader API issue could turn out to be different than in the US. In *Infopaq International A/S v. Danske Dagblades Forening* the CJEU held that copying short phrases could invite copyright liability so long as those fragments demonstrated the author's intellectual creation.[21]

At least as uncertain under EU law would be the situation with regard to the copyright assessment of grouping of methods as found in the Java APIs. It should first be reminded that the drafters of the Software Directive included preparatory design materials within the concept of computer programs. It follows that it would normally give rise to a copyright infringement for a program to be based on another program's preparatory design materials. This inclusion can be read as a revealing indication that the drafters of the Software Directive intended to grant copyright protection to the detailed SSO of the internal design of program writings.[22] Further guidance could be drawn from the CJEU holding that, while elements described in the SAS manual—including keywords, syntax and commands—could not be copyrighted individually, their "choice, sequence and combination" may warrant copyright protection as an intellectual creation of the author (para. 66-67) under general copyright law.

However, the functional character of APIs, being even stronger than with computer programs in general, would very often place them well below the originality threshold[23], and the general support in favour of interoperability expressed by the

---

[18] Christian Heinze, "Software als Schutzgegenstand des Europäischen Urheberrechts", (2011) 2 *Journal of Intellectual Property, Information Technology and E-Commerce Law* (jipitec), 97, 101, available at http://www.jipitec.eu/issues/jipitec-2-2-2011/3082.

[19] *Supra* (n.1), para. 3.13.

[20] Heinze (n.18), at 101.

[21] Case C-5/08, *Infopaq Int'l A/S v. Danske Dagblades Forening* [2009] ECR I-6569, paras. 37-51. See for a US/EU comparison on this issue Connor Moran "How Much is too Much? Copyright Protection of Short Portions of Text in the United States and European Union after *Infopaq International A/S v. Danske Dagblades*" (2011) 6 WASH. J.L. TECH. & ARTS 247, https://digital.lib.washington.edu/dspace-law/handle/1773.1/563.

[22] Heinze (n.18), at 101.

[23] Marly(n.14), at 779; Ashwin Van Rooijen,, "The Software Interface between Copyright and Competition Law: A Legal Analysis of Interoperability in Computer Programs", Kluwer Law International, 2010, at 79.

Software Directive could possibly present a further counterargument. As to a very tangible sign of that support, art. 6(1) of the Software Directive states that reverse engineering by way of decompilation of program object code is permitted solely when it the only way to obtain the information necessary to achieve interoperability with other programs. Thus, it could be held that copyright protection should be denied to the SSO of an API in case this hampers interoperability. A further question would be, however, if this applies *also* in case of interfaces reaching a level of imperfect interoperability, as it happened with the reproduction of the SSO of solely 37 Java APIs. In other words, the question could be raised whether the type of imperfect compatibility between the Java and the Android platforms achieved via the replication of the SSO of Java APIs would still be in line with the Software Directive's strong *pro*-interoperability stance.

REFERENCES

MORAN CONNOR, "How Much is too Much? Copyright Protection of Short Portions of Text in the United States and European Union after *Infopaq International A/S v. Danske Dagblades*" (2011) 6 *WASH. J.L. TECH. & ARTS* 247, available at https://digital.lib.washington.edu/dspace-law/handle/1773.1/563.

HEINZE CHRISTIAN, "Software als Schutzgegenstand des Europäischen Urheberrechts", (2011) *2 Journal of Intellectual Property, Information Technology and E-Commerce Law (jipitec)*, 97, available at http://www.jipitec.eu/issues/jipitec-2-2-2011/3082.

MARLY JOCHEN, "Der Schutzgegenstand des urheberrechtlichen Softwareschutzes," (2012) *GRUR*, 773.

SAMUELSON PAMELA, "Why Copyright Law Excludes Systems and Processes from the Scope of Its Protection," (2007) *85 Texas Law Review*, 1921.

SAMUELSON PAMELA, RANDALL DAVIES, MITCHELL D. KAPOR, and J. H. REICHMAN, "Manifesto on the Legal Protection of Computer Programs," (1994) 94 *COLUM. L. REV.*, 2308.

SAMUELSON PAMELA, THOMAS VINJE, and WILLIAM CORNISH, "Does Copyright Protection Under the EU Software Directive Extend to Program Behaviour, Languages and Interfaces?," (2012) 34 *European Intellectual Property Review*, 156.

VAN ROOIJEN ASHWIN, "The Software Interface between Copyright and Competition Law: A Legal Analysis of Interoperability in Computer Programs," (2010) Kluwer Law International.

WESTON SALLY, "Software Interfaces – Stuck in the Middle: The Relationship Between the Law and Software Interfaces in Regulating and Encouraging Interoperability" (2012) *International Review of Intellectual Property and Competition Law (IIC)*, 427.

36

Framing the *Conundrum* of Total Cost of Ownership of Open Source Software

Maha Shaikh
Warwick Business School
University of Warwick
Coventry, United Kingdom
Maha.shaikh@wbs.ac.uk

Tony Cornford
Dept. of Management
London School of Economics and Political Science
London, United Kingdom
T.cornford@lse.ac.uk

Abstract[1]— This paper reflects the results of phase I of our study on the total cost of ownership (TCO) of open source software adoption. Not only have we found TCO to be an intriguing issue but it is contentious, baffling and each company approaches it in a distinctive manner (and sometimes not at all). In effect it is a conundrum that needs unpacking before it can be explained and understood. Our paper discusses the components of TCO as total cost of ownership and total cost of acquisition (and besides). Using this broad dichotomy and its various components we then analyze our data to make sense of procurement decisions in relation to open source software in the public sector and private companies.

Index Terms—total cost of ownership, open source software, procurement.

I. INTRODUCTION

Total cost of ownership (TCO) is considered to be a fundamental issue when making software procurement decisions [1-4] in organizations yet this is an area that has received limited attention. In this paper we are concerned with TCO but more specifically in relation to open source software (OSS) adoption decisions by organizations. This adds yet another layer of complexity because the assessment of open source software procurement is not exactly the same as that for proprietary software [5]. Indeed, we find that by unpacking the idea of open source TCO we become more aware of the taken for granted in proprietary software procurement decisions. TCO has been defined as an understanding of 'the "true cost" of doing business with a particular supplier for a good or service' [6]. The idea of a 'true cost' and the ability to be able to assess it accurately, however is something most academics and practitioners would agree is not straightforward [7]. Thus we prefer a definition of TCO offered by Lerner and Schankerman [8] which distinguishes between different costs, and TCO is understood as the total cost of providing a functionality using one program. The proper accounting of cost should include total costs of procurement, management and support, associated hardware costs, and when one is thinking of changing software solutions, migration costs' (p107). In this definition we have a range of costs mentioned, all of which need attention before any true grasp of TCO of software can be reached.

Some authors claim that there is no such thing as '*the* cost of software' [8] implying that cost is a more multi-faceted issue which needs to be understood better. Thus, like all evaluation decisions TCO has a quantitative and qualitative element. In section 3 below we detail the various elements of each type of cost that we have noted from literature and from our data. We found this to be a recognized issue amongst practitioners in the public sector and the private. Most decisions taken on procurement in either sector are understandably based on cost but this is not the only factor and with open source software, we found that this is not even the most relevant. The larger concern for companies eager to adopt open source software was reduced vendor lock-in, and what companies understood as 'value for money' (see Fig 1 below).

Lerner and Schankerman [8], with their distinctions in costs, indicate the conundrum of TCO. Companies are becoming more aware of these issues but the smaller ones do not have the resources to actually carry out a full detailed TCO study. How does a company assess the softer costs [9] surrounding software procurement especially when the software is open source (a relatively less familiar category for many companies)? It is important to make sense of the categories of cost and exactly what they entail to better manage them and make better informed decisions.

A. Conundrum of TCO of OSS

Literature in the area of TCO provides some useful models of cost evaluation [10]. What interests us in this study is not only the quantifiable costs but the more amorphous expense that occurs at the start, operation and even migration away from the software adoption. Business analysts [11-13] in this area have made note of the many possibilities that open source offers companies [14] but again these are hard to quantify, and often for smaller companies this is a consideration for the future. Most small companies that adopt open source software do so with the intention of cutting back on license costs (as the license cost of OSS is zero or close to it) [10, 15]. However, the

---

[1] An amended version of this paper was first presented at the OSS 2011 Conference in Salvador, Brazil.

total cost of ownership is not the same as the total cost of acquisition, or the cost of operation, and this is the space we want to explore with our study. This categorization is necessary as this has temporal consequences for adoption of software.

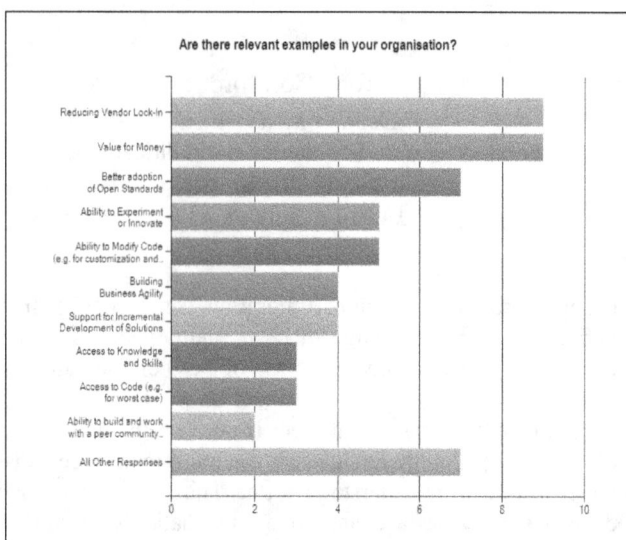

Fig. 1. This figure shows the various factors companies in our survey considered when making a decision to move to open source, and the relative weight of each factor.

The total cost of acquisition usually refers to the costs that are needed to bring the software to the actual point of use, so theoretically it includes the cost of software (buying it). The total cost of operation is more nuanced a cost but very relevant in the open source domain where companies need to adjust their TCO models to take into account the different areas of expense that OSS involves. Operational costs refer to the policies in place in companies that encourage and aid open source adoption, and very importantly, clear and structured TCO assessments before making procurement decisions.

In this paper we explore the various forms of costs that are necessary for companies and the public sector to explore in detail before making any procurement decisions, but especially those related to open source as this is a relatively new concept for them and different in that the license cost is very low yet other costs seem to mount (but are often ignored and not understood).

II. METHODOLOGY

This study is structured to take place in two phases. This paper reflects some of the results from phase I which includes a survey of twenty-five questions. These questions cover the basics of the company size, name and focus, but then go on to ask some very detailed questions about the various applications that are open source, why they were chosen, if they replaced proprietary software, was any difference in cost experienced, and finally, what prompted this change or need to adopt open source software. The responses to the survey, especially to the last question will be fed into an interview guide. This then takes us to phase II where we aim to conduct between 35-40 in-depth interviews. Access in a number of organizations that responded to the survey has already been negotiated and phase II will take place over the summer of 2011.

A. Phase I - Survey

Phase 1 involved the creation of the survey which was based on literature and documentation that helped to understand TCO models used in companies. The survey was set up for access in two ways, document form (available in odt, pdf and doc formats) and an online version set up in SurveyMonkey. The aim of this study is to make sense of adoption of open source software by both private companies and public sector organizations. Though funded by the UK Cabinet Office to assess and evaluate the costs and issues involved in open source adoption by government agencies we decided that a more sound methodology would involve a balanced mix of commercial and public sector organizations. Public sector organizations are not profit orientated yet there is much to learn from private companies and their manner of dealing with open source. The larger idea here is the level of experience and comfort that private companies bring to open source adoption which is sorely lacking in the public sector. There are some exemplary cases of open source adoption by the public sector like the Extremadura case in Spain [16, 17] but there are far more 'success' stories of open source adoption by commercial companies [18-21]. The factors that encourage private companies to adopt open source software, especially considering most business models of such adoption indicate that the software itself does not lead to value creation or capture directly [22-25], make some of the lessons translatable across both sectors.

The survey was put online for a period of two months (and is still online but for the sake of this paper we only took into account the surveys completed in the first two months) and we received twenty-four responses. We also received seven paper based surveys sent back to us as scanned documents via email. This made a total of thirty-one surveys. We had set the survey to ensure that details of the respondent was a required category. This was done to be able to filter out any responses that were biased, duplicate or simply not completed with any seriousness. Of the 24 online surveys two were filled in by people calling themselves 'test' and 'anonymous'. We discounted the results from both these surveys. We also had two incomplete surveys online. Incomplete surveys were those where some questions were skipped. As this exercise was carried out as a precursor and data gathering exercise more for the interest of creating a strong and clear interview guide for phase II we accepted the results of the incomplete surveys. Phase II is where the researchers involved in this study hope to gain a more detailed understanding of TCO models and the decision-making process in organizations so it was felt that so long as the surveys were recognized to be valid (not anonymous or biased) and useful (filled in 75% of the survey and added some non-mandatory comments that helped us to evaluate the experience of the company with open source) we would include the results to help shape the interview guide for phase II.

B. Data Analysis

Of the total surveys we received the majority of them were filled in by small to medium sized private companies (44%). Small to medium sized enterprises included all those with a number of employees ranging between 1-100. We had 24% of the surveys completed by employees of large, and in many cases global companies (employees ranging from 101 and above). Public sector replies made 32% of the total. In phase II we intend to cover a larger portion of the public sector.

The survey had a number of questions where respondents were asked to add comments or spell out the category of 'other' in more detail. Responses to such questions gave rise to some very interesting issues which will become a part of the interview guide and informed the researchers involved.

Phase I has given rise to some very interesting findings. The main ideas the respondents focused on included the lack of maturity level of open source software, license confusions and lack of knowledge about the implications of various open source licenses. Other ideas which arose were somewhat more surprising, most organizations do not even attempt a TCO study before making procurement decisions because of the expense such studies involve. The models used to assess TCO are also more suited for proprietary software and companies are not comfortable or skilled to tweak them for open source. And lastly, there is no policy in most companies for open source adoption. These decisions are made more ad-hoc and usually based on pragmatic decisions of use and need rather than cost.

III. ANALYSIS AND DISCUSSION

The survey results are very interesting and we only have space to share some of the key ideas that emerged. These ideas include the importance of liberty [15] and flexibility (reduced vendor lock-in) provided by open source to companies and the public sector, that long term costs vary far more across companies considering their size and experience with open source, short term costs are slightly higher, that most companies choose a combination of open source and proprietary software where their decisions are based on pragmatism and need rather than questions of openness.

In this section we take these broad themes and frame them in relation to another interesting dimension that we noted from our data, that of a more fine-tuned TCO categorization than has been offered so far by other studies. We found that the cost categories were not limited to two broad ones, cost of acquisition and cost of operation, but instead we recognized two other very key cost factors that companies are beginning to take very seriously in relation to open source software procurement decisions – cost of adoption and exit costs (see Table 1).

A. Cost of Adoption

The cost of adoption, we found, concerns all the relevant expenses involved with the broad idea of adoption such as the learning necessary when you adopt open source for the first time or for a new part of the stack (see Table 2). Very importantly it also includes interoperability costs which many companies surprisingly ignore even though this is a feature of proprietary software as well. The difference with open source is that some respondents stated that they feel they can make the necessary adjustments because the code is open, yet as we are becoming more aware, there is a steep learning curve with all software not created in-house. Upgrades are a growing concern for companies with open source because most open source software tends to adapt and be changed more frequently than proprietary. Of course the choice to upgrade is with the user yet interoperability can also become a problem if one software is upgraded but other applications and infrastructure are not.

TABLE I. DIFFERENT CATEGORIES OF TCO, AND WHAT EACH INVOLVES

Categories of TCO			
Cost of adoption	Cost of software	Cost of operation	Exit costs
Learning	Initial purchase price	Formal TCO assessment	Migration costs
Interoperability	Monetary costs of set-up	TCO policy	Re-training
Support services	Customization expense	Cost of evaluating software (tinkering)	Switching costs
Training	Software scaling cost		
Access to upgrades			

B. Exit Costs

Exit costs are yet a more intriguing idea. Respondents agreed that this aspect was the most ignored and yet it formed a very large part of the overall TCO of open source adoption. Table 2 outlines the areas where the costs with open source were considered to be the lowest but take note of the 'other' category in Table 2 and Figure 2.

TABLE II. AREAS AND APPLICATIONS OF OPEN SOURCE SOFTWARE WHICH SAVED MONEY FOR ORGANIZATIONS

Which OSS saved your organization money?				
	Agree	Agree somewhat	Completely disagree	No change in expense - same
Applications:	75.0%	12.5%	0.0%	6.3%
Enterprise systems	71.4%	0.0%	0.0%	0.0%
Vertical/line of business	58.3%	0.0%	0.0%	0.0%
Desktop	84.6%	7.7%	0.0%	0.0%
System's Development	71.4%	7.1%	0.0%	7.1%
Infrastructure:	84.6%	7.7%	0.0%	0.0%
OS Platforms	88.2%	11.8%	0.0%	0.0%
Application Servers	84.6%	0.0%	0.0%	7.7%
Web services	93.3%	0.0%	0.0%	0.0%
Networking	86.7%	6.7%	0.0%	0.0%
Database	86.7%	0.0%	0.0%	13.3%
Other	72.6%	0.0%	0.0%	0.0%

Upon reading the comments added by the respondents it was evident that though open source saved the organization money there were costs that had been ignored and ill-understood.

Exit costs include all the expenses of switching from one software to another, various interoperability expenses, costs related to legacy systems, retraining staff and initial teething issue costs. This is an area where at least at present companies feel that open source costs are higher and not clear at all. The low license costs with open source software, according to the respondents though very real can become misleading because companies simply begin to base their decisions on that cost alone and dismiss any other factor.

C. Vendor Lock-in and Lock-out

Vendor lock-in though a real problem with proprietary software is less so with open source. This may well be a real consideration yet what we note from our study so far is that expertise of the software (be it open source or otherwise) and a lack of good documentation which is a problem with open source often becomes a *lock-out*. Companies feel discouraged from adopting any software they cannot control, but also cannot obtain comprehensive services and troubleshooting. The idea of reaching out to an unknown community [26] has a romantic appeal but is not practical. Indeed, such promises spread FUD about open source adoption and lead to lock-out because companies avoid anything they are not familiar with. It is easy enough in theory to take code and customize it yet as many respondents noted this is not so in practice. They are forced to hire experts and look for support to communities outside the company. This is a drain on their resources and an expense that was not considered by the decision takers, even if a TCO assessment was carried out before procurement decisions were taken.

D. Temporal Element of TCO

Another key theme that arose from our survey data was that of cost temporality. Of the four costs outlined in Table 1 the cost of adoption and exit costs are relatively quite high for open source software. This is even more marked with the added complexity of the size and experience of the organization. If the company is large *and* experienced with open source then these two costs are often well-understood and thus less expensive. Large companies can diversify and absorb costs better than smaller companies and this is largely true for the public sector as well. Smaller organizations however usually jump on the open source bandwagon with the naive idea that this will prove cheaper. They have also not undertaken a TCO analysis and if they are not experienced with open source it was then found that the expense of open source surprised many. In some cases, especially in the public sector (coupled with issues of poor interoperability) we have seen a return to proprietary software. Phase II of our study will include this local authority as a full case study to better explore the problems, issues and dilemmas that forced it to return to closed source software adoption.

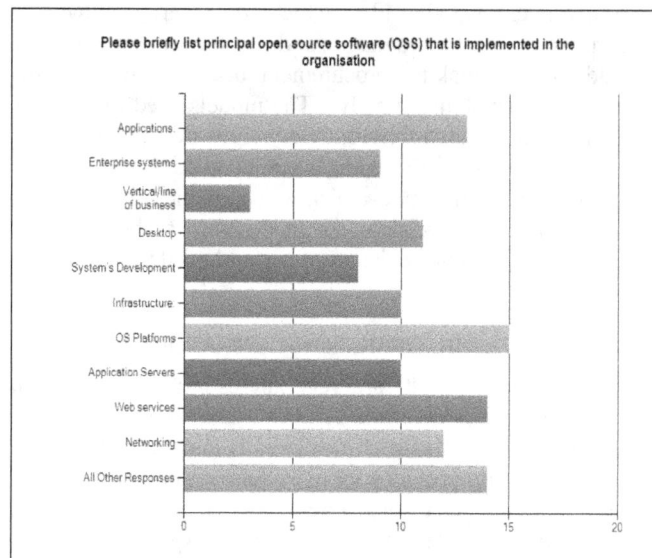

Fig. 2. This figure shows the various open source software concentration in implementation in the different organizations.

E. Pragmatism and the Idea of Value

Most companies, like software developers and hackers work on the basis of pragmatism. If something is good enough and not broken then it will be continued to be used. Open source requires some experience and practice and very key, the licenses involved with open source need good skills and expertise, something most small companies do not have the resources for and the public sector simply does not consider. In effect if something is good enough then change is considered problematic and unnecessary. In the public sector in the UK we have found that local authorities are beginning to gravitate towards open source simply because of the lower costs promised by open source (due to the recession), however a better understanding of the benefits of open source is needed. The idea of where the *value* lies in open source software adoption is the needed. And by value we do not mean a monetary value (though it does include this category) we refer to the softer side of benefits – that of flexibility, openness, freedoms, ability to tweak and customize and along with open standards and open data – a far more open and accessible software environment. This is where the true benefits and cost reductions will come in the future.

The real value in open source adoption is clearly the collaborative co-creative ideology and spirit it encourages. This in turn leads to value creation, innovation, and a stronger ecosystem [27].

IV. CONCLUSION

This paper maps the initial stages of our study of the total cost of ownership of open source software adoption. The analysis provides some interesting answers to broad questions about cost but more importantly it raises relevant questions about the rather enigmatic quality of assessing the total cost of software, especially open source software. It is a conundrum as most companies lack experience with open source and more to the point, a slightly different understanding of 'value for money' is needed. The actual monetary cost of open source software adoption in many cases is not unlike that of proprietary software but it is the liberties, flexibility and control that it provides that draws companies and the public sector towards it.

However, there is much detail yet to be teased out in this amorphous area, and during the course of this study we hope to be able to show more clearly where the large part of the costs lie with open source software adoption, exactly where and how they are distinctive in comparison to proprietary software, what strategies and practices the public sector and companies can employ to make more effective use of the unique qualities of open source so that the software can yield a stronger feeling of 'value for money'. Indeed, can we go so far as to suggest that open source software adoption is an idea that the public sector not only needs to toy with seriously but in fact it will prove more effective, valuable, cheaper and necessary in the future? We aim to be able to provide a more nuanced answer to this and other questions at the end of our study, and encourage other researchers to explore such aspects because we feel that public sector adoption of open source has the potential to have real influence on open government strategies [28], open standards, and open data.

ACKNOWLEDGMENT

We would like to thank The UK Cabinet Office, OpenForum Europe and other organizations that made this research possible. The aim of this research is to assess the various costs and value of open source adoption by the public sector and private organizations.

REFERENCES

[1] L. M. Ellram, "A Taxonomy of Total Cost of Ownership Model," *Journal of Business Logistics,* vol. 15, pp. 171-191, 1994.

[2] L. M. Ellram, "Total cost of ownership an analysis approach for purchasing. ," *Journal of Physical Distribution and Logistics* vol. 25, pp. 4-23, 1995.

[3] L. M. Ellram and S. P. Siferd, "Total Cost of Ownership: A Key Concept in Strategic Cost Management Decisions," *Journal of Business Logistics,* vol. 19, pp. 55-84, 1998.

[4] K. Hurkens, W. v. d. Valk, and F. Wynstra, "Total Cost of Ownership in the Services Sector: A Case Study," *The Journal of Supply Chain Management,* vol. 42, pp. 27-37, 2006.

[5] A. MacCormack, "Evaluating Total Cost of Ownership for Software Platforms: Comparing Apples, Oranges, and Cucumbers," AEI-Brookings Joint Center for Regulatory Studies Series 2003.

[6] L. M. Ellram, "A Framework for Total Cost of Ownership," *The International Journal of Logistics Management,* vol. 4, pp. 46-60, 1993.

[7] M. J. F. Wouters, J. C. Anderson, and F. Wynstra, "The Adoption of Total Cost of Ownership for Sourcing Decisions - A Structural Equations Analysis," *Accounting, Organizations and Society,* vol. 30, pp. 167-191, 2005.

[8] J. Lerner and M. Schankerman, *The Comingled Code: Open Source and Economic Development*. Hong Kong: MIT Press, 2010.

[9] L. P. Carr and C. D. Ittner, "Measuring the Cost of Ownership," *Journal of Cost Management,* vol. 6, pp. 42-51, 1992.

[10] B. Russo and G. Succi, "A Cost Model of Open Source Software Adoption," *IJOSSP,* pp. 60-82, 2009.

[11] R. Sutor, "Managing open source adoption in your IT organization," 2009.

[12] R. Gallopino, "Open Source TCO: Total Cost of Ownership and the Fermat's Theorem," 2009.

[13] R. Burkhardt, "Seven Predictions for Open Source in 2009," 2008.

[14] D. A. Wheeler, "Why Open Source Software / Free Software (OSS/FS, FLOSS, or FOSS)? Look at the Numbers!," 2007.

[15] S. Phipps, "Open Source Procurement: Subscriptions," in *ComputerWorldUK*, 2011.

[16] P. Zuliani and G. Succi, "Migrating public administrations to open source software," in *E-society 2004 IADIS International Conference*, Avila, Spain, 2004, pp. 829-832.

[17] P. ZULIANI and G. SUCCI, "An Experience of Transition to Open Source Software in Local Authorities," in *E-challenges on Software Engineering*, Vienna, Austria, 2004

[18] J. Dinkelacker, P. Garg, R. Miller, and D. Nelson, "Progressive Open Source," Hewlett-Packard, Palo Alto, California HPL-2001-233, September 28th, 2001.

[19] L. Dahlander, "Penguin in a newsuit: a tale of how de novo entrants emerged to harness free and open source software communities," *Industrial and Corporate Change* vol. 16, pp. 913-943, 2007.

[20] B. Fitzgerald, "The Transformation of Open Source Software," *MIS Quarterly,* vol. 30, pp. 587-598, September, 2006.

[21] S. O'Mahony, F. C. Diaz, and E. Mamas, "IBM and Eclipse (A)," *Harvard Business Review Case Study,* vol. December 16, 2005.

[22] J. West and S. Gallagher, "Challenges of Open Innovation: The Paradox of Firm Investment in Open Source Software," *R&D Management,* vol. 36, pp. 315-328, 2006.

[23] J. West, "How Open is Open Enough? Melding Proprietary and Open Source Platform Strategies," *Research Policy,* vol. 32, pp. 1259-1285, 2003.

[24] A. Osterwalder, Y. Pigneur, and C. L. Tucci, "Clarifying Business Models: Origins, Present, and Future of the Concept," *Communications of the Association for Information Systems,* vol. 15, pp. 1-40, 2005.

[25] S. L. Vargo and R. F. Lusch, "Evolving to a New Dominant Logic for Marketing," *Journal of Marketing* vol. 68, pp. 1-17, 2004.

[26] P. Agerfalk and B. Fitzgerald, "Outsourcing to an Unknown Workforce: Exploring Opensourcing as a Global Sourcing Strategy," *MIS Quarterly,* vol. 32, pp. 385-400, 2008.

[27] M. Shaikh and T. Cornford, "Understanding Commercial Open Source as Product and Service Innovation," in *2011 Academy of Management Annual Meeting,* San Antonio, Texas, USA, 2011.

[28] B. S. Noveck, "Defining Open Government," 2011. Address: http://cairns.typepad.com/blog/2011/04/whats-in-a-name-open-gov-we-gov-gov-20-collaborative-government.html

Consumer Trust, Education and Empowerment: The Open Story

Altsitsiadis Efthymios
Research Center of Marketing and Consumer Science
Katholieke Universiteit Leuven
Belgium
efthymios.a@gmail.com

Abstract—Conventional policy making suggests the need to boost trust within supply and user markets, to educate users to better understand the underlying risks, and finally to empower the users so that their informed decisions help shape a better ICT market that will benefit society. This paper relies on recent scientific evidence and attempts to connect the loosely connected dots above into a slightly less conventional story.

Index Terms—Consumer, trust, education, empowerment.

I. INTRODUCTION

The Information and Communications Technology (ICT) market, despite its undoubtedly remarkable development, still faces a number of challenges, many of which can be associated with or traced back to the lack of trust, education and empowerment. These three concepts, long present in the ICT agenda are typically viewed from a rather monotonous, given perspective, one that ignores the finer constructs and the limitations that seem to exist.

This paper relies on evidence from the MIS and consumer sciences to reveal some common preconceptions and to share simple considerations for the impact of these three multi-dimensional and potentially interdependent concepts on ICTs.

II. ABOUT TRUST

Trust is the key-or so do many leading ICT experts declare quite often in their public addresses and publications. This is the one catch-phrase that most stakeholders, background and point of interest aside would likely find easy to agree with, regardless of whether the discussion is on Cloud Computing, Open Innovation, procurement or almost any other topic in which one side needs to somehow collaborate with another. The European Commission (EC) recognizes the importance of trust and stresses in its Digital Agenda *the need to create technology neutral ways of enhancing trust and confidence by strengthening citizens' rights*.

Indeed, trust is central for successful economic exchange [1] and in particular for economic prosperity in post-modern societies, where an increased emphasis on technologies heightens a perception of complex and uncertain economic relationships [2]. Determining whom to trust and whom to distrust is a major decision in impersonal IT-enabled exchanges [3]. Research on trust has been in the spotlight in the MIS field (among other fields, like international and relational marketing, strategy and so on) in the past few decades, covering a wide range of trust-related topics based on a multitude of theories from sociology and psychology to economics [4]. We will start with some basic definitions and then move on to analyze some key aspects of trust relevant to both research and policy making.

A. Trust basics

The extensive literature across the various disciplines that deals with trust reveals the rich and diverse multilevel construct of trust in terms of types, dimensions, models. Mayer et al define trust as *the willingness of a party (the trustor) to be vulnerable to the actions of another party (the trustee) based on the expectation that the trustee will perform a particular action important to the trustor, irrespective of the ability to monitor or control that other party [5]*.

This generalized expectancy held by an individual that the word of another can be relied on, highlights the importance of confidence. Confidence on the part of the trusting party results from the firm belief that the trustworthy party is reliable and has high integrity, which are associated with such qualities as consistent, competent, honest, fair, responsible, helpful, and benevolent [6]. 'Willingness' denotes the behavioral basis; this behavioral intention is a critical facet of trust's conceptualization because "if one believes that a partner is trustworthy without being willing to rely on that partner, trust is limited [7]. These dimensions and their interactions are merely a part of a deeper multilevel construct; for the scope of this position paper though, we will focus on the aspects that we consider more relevant to ICT policy making.

B. Trust varies across borders, cultures and institutional boundaries

Policy makers and ICT stakeholders tend to view trust as an etic concept, assuming the common viewpoint of trust as culture-general, universal concept. The evidence from the literature implies limitations associated with this assumption: the levels and degree of trust differ across international borders [8-10] but also both the nature of trust and the institutional and cultural support for trust can vary across different national contexts [11] and organizational boundaries [12]. This intersection of different levels and meanings of trust challenges our traditional view of trust symmetry along partners, and is believed to have an impact on international collaborations that should not be ignored [11].

The differences in trust across societies have both institutional and cultural determinants. The institutional basis of trust - comprised of the legal, political, and social systems that support the monitoring and sanctioning of social behavior - is perhaps the most critical determinant of trust [13]). The role of culture in shaping trust has been examined in numerous studies, mostly within Hofstede's Individualism-Collectivism framework (e.g. Huff & Kelley [14], who showed that a higher level of propensity to trust and higher external trust, exists in business relations in the US than in Asia) and cultural distance, providing ample evidence that the foundations of trust differ across cultures [15].

The European Union has 27 member states with distinct cultural characteristics and varying levels of baseline institutional trust, all of which need to collaborate both together and globally in the highly ambiguous and dynamic environment of ICTs. In conjunction to this reality, the scientific findings cast doubts on whether our innate 'etic' approach to trust is efficient and whether one-size-fits-all legislative interventions will have an effect on boosting trust. Cultural, institutional and organizational barriers could also offer partial explanation to pressing trust issues (such as EU-US trust in Clouds, open Vs proprietary procurement) and can ground the reasons for a more open approach to trust, rather than a purely regulatory one.

C. Trust, Distrust and Gender

Trust related research in Information Systems recently made an important methodological step forward. Drawing from the social neuroscience discipline (neuroeconomics, neuropsychology and neuromarketing), MIS researchers employed functional neuroimaging tools (fMRI) to complement traditional phychometric measures of trust, wielding breakthrough results [4]. In the context of impersonal exchanges, strong empirical evidence supports that:

- Trust and distrust activate different brain areas and have different effects [16]

- Most of the brain areas that encode trustworthiness differ between women and men [17]

Dimoka's [16] results can help explain why trust and distrust are distinct constructs associated with different neurological processes - trust seems probably more cognitive and calculative in nature, while distrust is more emotional in nature. Riedl et al [17] results reopen the discussion for gender differences in trust. These studies provide new insights that put our current understanding of trust into question. Perhaps even more important is the fact that this new measurement approach opens avenues for future research, calling for a reexamination of the nature, dimensionality, distinction and relative effects of multiple IS constructs, like satisfaction, or the different nature of the many types of risks in outsourcing contracts [4].

We should embrace the transformative developments in MIS research in two ways: utilize the new insights to enhance our understanding of trust and support new research down this path as to increase our knowledge on other, perhaps even more important concepts.

D. Do we need more trust or less?

Trust is placed next to security in most of the European policy workings, implying a strong correlation among the two concepts in the beliefs of EU policy makers. The Digital Agenda suggests that *'Europeans will not embrace technology they don't trust'* it is safe and secure. Trust and privacy are also very closely linked and it would probably not be excessive to suggest that privacy and security are dominating the agenda on trust, while a strong, almost unilateral emphasis on trustworthiness is apparent throughout the EC documents and initiatives (e.g. Trust in Digital Life). The European Commission defines 'Trustworthy ICT' as *secure, reliable and resilient to attacks and operational failures; guaranteeing quality of service; protecting user data; ensuring privacy and providing usable and trusted tools to support the user in his security management* [18].

Employing our common sense, it is rather safe to assume that users will place their trust on safe ICT solutions that respect their privacy. Recent findings from the marketing discipline, however, show that online trust is perhaps more elusive and not always linearly rational or predictable. In an interesting empirical study published in a leading marketing journal, Bart et al [19] tested their conceptual model that links Web site and consumer characteristics, online trust, and behavioral intent. They tested a number of different potential online trust drivers (security, privacy, brand strength, navigation and presentation and so on) over different Website category factors.

Surprisingly perhaps, security was not found to have a dominant effect on any website category (even on those that the authors expected e.g. financial services). The authors' explanation is that *perhaps security is so basic for all sites that it does not explain any variance in the presence of other drivers* [19]. Furthermore, it was found that collectively, navigation and presentation, advice, and brand strength are more influential predictors of online trust than are privacy and security.

Although the paper was limited in examining the Internet, the authors argue that many of the same factors are present in other channels, such as e-mail, telephone, direct mail, and physical store formats. At a broad level, the evidence implies that trying to boost online consumer trust by focusing on security will probably have limited efficiency. More importantly, these findings imply a discrepancy between what governments and users tend to believe – On the one hand governments and industry give significant weight to security, and for a good reason as security issues in ICT are everything but negligible, on the other hand user trust seems to shape rather independently, treating security as a baseline minimum that is considered as given.

Since security risks are real and user trust seems to be influenced by other variables, it can be inferred that users might be failing to acknowledge the importance of security and thus behaving risky. In this situation, users would probably be better off if they were less trusting. Since lowering trust is not really an option, we could take a different step: educate consumers on these security issues and how to safely make decisions in the complex electronic world.

III. ABOUT CONSUMER EDUCATION

As the conclusive paragraph above suggests, there could be an issue of 'overconfidence' which could be associated to the lack of knowledge or awareness of the actual risks on a significant part of the users. EC vice-president Kroes highlights the risks of stolen data, profile misuse and purloined identities [20], most of which could be at least partially mitigated if users behaved online in a more safe/informed manner (e.g. read the legal terms, use an updated antimalware software and so on). Educating consumers is believed by many experts to be a necessity when it comes to risky online behavior [21]. Based on the wide belief that when a user is made aware of the risks he will act by changing his behavior accordingly, education, in its wide sense, seems like an appropriate tool for intervention.

The evidence regarding influencing consumer behavior, however, reveals a rather more complicated and less encouraging picture. A lot of money has been poured into intervention programs (including integrated ones that surpass simple education initiatives) aiming at eradicating undesirable behavior and/or promoting desirable behavior. Although some of these attempts have met with success, interventions typically yield very modest results [22], often only in the short run or for subpopulations that are not the most needing beneficiaries [23]. Most disturbing, some interventions have even been suspected to have had ironic effects. Even worse is that our knowledge about what works and why, is anecdotal, and hence not readily replicable [22]. Two major gaps plague behavioral change interventions: the gap between the lab and the field [22], and the gap between intentions and behavior [24]. As consumer behavior tends to become ever more complex [25], these gaps can only deepen, so it seems.

The EC is quite aware of these gaps and in the mean time appreciates the importance of unlocking consumer behavior for policy making [24]. Based on their own exercise findings [25] the Commission stresses that 'Understanding motivations and the main determinants behind consumer related behavior is essential for policy-making'. There are two issues here though. The EC does not recognize online (or ICT related) behavior as a potential application area, limiting its potential application to more traditional areas like food [24], instead of working with ICT stakeholders to collaborate on the topic. In addition, the EC seems to take a step back to its overall approach on consumer behavior. The 'European Consumer Agenda' emphasizes 'enhancing knowledge' as a main objective for 2020 [26], yet the envisaged steps are rather limited to raising awareness on consumer rights and to raising consumer participation through knowledge and capacities (e.g. consumer center networks), leaving the premise of actual behavior rather unaddressed.

Conclusively, as the evidence suggests that education is not enough to solve the issues at hand, we need to turn our attention to other solutions that offer sustainable and transferable results – complementary to education we could empower consumers.

IV. ABOUT CONSUMER EMPOWERMENT

The 2007-2013 EU Consumer Strategy set the primary aim of empowering EU consumers to help them maximize their welfare as well as to drive competition and innovation. According to the EC [27], empowered consumers make optimal decisions by understanding their own preferences and the choices available to them. They know their rights, recognize when these have been breached and if so, complain and seek redress when necessary. Consumer empowerment is also a priority of the EC's Digital Agenda, which stresses that *'the digital era should be about empowerment and emancipation'* [28]. Empowered consumers should be both confident and knowledgeable and feel protected.

The idea of empowering ICT consumers with the necessary skills, knowledge and assertiveness, along with the necessary protection, rules and institutional support should be enough to offer a sustainable solution to the issues at hand, while in the mean time, their empowered autonomous choices would inject innovation through better stimulation of the competition benefiting the ICT sector in total.

Although this situation would probably sit well with any rational policy maker, the evidence once more seems to blur this ideal setting. One assumption commonly held by those who seek to empower consumers is that consumers will perceive any increase in control as a benefit: *Helping consumers choose what they want, when they want it, and on their own terms, is obviously a benefit* [29]. Wathieu et al [30] consider this generalization too crude and offer examples where greater perceptions of empowerment may also entail costs for consumer, further suggesting directions for a fuller understanding of both positive and negative consequences of increased consumer control.

The evidence from the marketing literature on whether consumer empowerment increases satisfaction is mixed, to the knowledge of the EC [31]. The EC launched in 2010 a Eurobarometer survey on consumer empowerment with perhaps surprising results on this specific subject. The survey showed that consumers who feel more confident seem not to read completely and carefully terms and conditions when signing contracts, while equivocally they seem to be more interested in information on their rights as compared to non empowered consumers [31]. The European Consumer Agenda nevertheless, emphasizes the (unconditional) need to boost consumer confidence [26].

The short analysis above brings out that our current understanding of consumer power is not sufficient or clear to support the claim that empowerment is always a good thing and that will lead to a desired political outcome. ICTs are both an enabler (giving tremendous control to the user) and a field of application (empowered users skilled to navigate safely and taking advantage of the digital market) of consumer empowerment. There is no doubt that there is great value down this path, but also that we need more upstream research on the actual effects of empowerment. At minimum, policy makers should be aware that consumer empowerment might come with side-effects.

V. DISCUSSION

The paper attempts to place under one frame three concepts that are broadly used in the ICT agenda, and revisit each of them under the light of the newest scientific developments from the MIS and consumer disciplines. The analysis demonstrates the underlying dimensionality and interdependence and questions the dominant thinking of conventional policy. Consumer trust, education and empowerment are not univocal concepts and European ICT policy can benefit by realizing its consumer-relevancy and by embracing innovative consumer insights.

One of the limitations of this study is that it only entertains the usual user-centric semantics. Interesting questions arise when one places governments as the centerpiece of this discussion: Do policy makers trust citizens? Is governmental trust shaped rationally? Do governments learn and behave as empowered consumers themselves?

Governmental trust in society is more likely to be reflected in 'light touch' approaches to legislation. An 'educated' government would mean that policy makers not only build their intentions based on good knowledge but also act rationally on them. Finally, governments themselves can act as empowered consumers by applying true open competitive choice in their own procurement procedures.

REFERENCES

[1] P. Zak and S. Knack. Trust and Growth. The Economic Journal, Vol. 111, No. 470 (Apr., 2001), pp. 295-321

[2] Resnick, Paul and R. Zeckhauser. "Trust Among Strangers in Internet Transactions: Empirical Analysis of eBay's Reputation System." The Economics of the Internet and E-Commerce. Michael R. Baye, editor. Volume 11 of Advances in Applied Microeconomics. Amsterdam, Elsevier Science. 2002. pp. 127-157.

[3] V. L. Smith,"Constructivist and Ecological Rationality in Economics," *American Economic Review* (93:3), pp. 465-508.2003

[4] I. Benbasat, D. Gefen, P. Pavlou, "Introduction to the special issue on novel perspectives on Trust in Information Systems." *MIS Quarterly Vol. 34 No. 2 pp. 367-371/June 2010*

[5] R.C. Mayer, J. H. Davis, F. D. Schoorman, "An integrative model of organizational trust." Acad. Management Rev. 20(3) 709-734.1995

[6] R. M. Morgan and S. D. Hunt. "The Commitment-Trust Theory of Relationship Marketing." The Journal of Marketing, Vol. 58, No. 3 (Jul., 1994), pp. 20-38

[7] C. Moorman, R. Deshpande, and G. Zaltman, "Factors Affecting Trust in Market Research Relation-ships," Journal of Marketing, 57 (January), 81-101.1993

[8] F. Fukuyama, "Trust: The Social Virtues and the Creation of Prosperity", The Free Press: New York. 1995

[9] T. Yamagishi, K.S. Cook and M. Watabe, "Uncertainty, trust, and commitment formation in the United States and Japan", American Journal of Sociology 104(1): 165–194.1998

[10] J.H. Dyer and W.J. Chu, "The role of trustworthiness in reducing transaction costs and improving performance: empirical evidence from the United States, Japan, and Korea", Organization Science 14(1): 57–68.2003

[11] S Zaheer and A Zaheer. "Trust across borders" Journal of International Business Studies (2006) 37, 21–29

[12] A. Madhok, "Revisiting multinational firms' tolerance for joint ventures: a trust-based approach", Journal of International Business Studies 26(1): 117–137.1995

[13] L.G. Zucker, "Production of Trust: Institutional Sources of Economic Structure, 1840–1920", in B.M. Staw and L.L. Cummings (eds.) Research in Organizational Behavior, Vol. 8, JAI Press Inc.: Greenwich, CT, pp: 53–111.1986

[14] L. Huff and L. Kelley, "Levels of organizational trust in individualist versus collectivist societies: a seven-nation study", Organization Science 14(1): 81–90.2003

[15] C. Lane, "The social regulation of inter-firm relations in Britain and Germany: market rules, legal norms and technical standards", Cambridge Journal of Economics 21(2): 197–215.1997

[16] A. Dimoka, "What does the brain tell us about trust and distrust? Evidence from a functional neuroimaging study." *MIS Quarterly Vol. 34 No. 2 pp. 373-396/June 2010*

[17] R. Riedl, M. Hubert and P. Kenning, "Are there neural gender differences in online trust? An MRI study on the perceived trustworthiness of eBay offers." *MIS Quarterly Vol. 34 No. 2 pp. 397-428/June 2010*

[18] *European Commission. 2012. ICT Work Programme 2013*

[19] Y. Bart, V. Shankar. F. Sultan and G. Urban, "Are the drivers and role of online trust the same for all Web Sites and consumers? A large scale exploratory empirical study" *Journal of Marketing* Vol. 69 (October 2005), 133–152

[20] A Report of the advisory board RISEPTIS. Trust in information society

[21] Openforum Academy, 2012, Who do you trust with your data in the cloud? www.openforumacademy.org/library/round-table/Round Table Report _ Who do you Trust with your Data in the cloud_.pdf

[22] WHO, 2008, Behaviour change strategies and health: the role of health systems. *Regional committee for Europe-58th session.*

[23] Van sluijs et al. 2003, *Beh.Med.J*

[24] EC, Directorate – General for health and consumers. Consumer Behaviour: the road to effective policy-making.

[25] Future Challenges Paper: 2009-2014. http://ec.europa.eu/dgs/health_consumer/future_challenges/future_challenges_paper.pdf

[26] European Commission. 2012. A European Consumer Agenda - Boosting confidence and growth http://ec.europa.eu/consumers/strategy/docs/consumer_agenda_2012_en.pdf

[27] European Commission.COMMISSION STAFF WORKING PAPER Consumer Empowerment in the EU

http://ec.europa.eu/consumers/consumer_empowerment/docs/swd_consumer_empowerment_eu_en.pdf

[28] European Commission. 2010. A Digital Agenda for Europe
http://eur-lex.europa.eu/LexUriServ/LexUriServ.do?uri=COM:2010:0245:FIN:EN:PDF

[29] D. Kreps,"A Representation Theorem for Preference for Flexibility," Econometrica, 47, 565-577. 1979

[30] L. Wathieu, L. Brenner, Z. Carmon, A. Chattopadhyay, K. Wertenbroch, A. Drolet, J. Gourville, A.V. Muthukrishnan, N. Novemsky, R. Ratner, G. Wu, "Consumer Control and Empowerment: A Primer." Marketing Letters, Vol. 13, No. 3, Choice Modeling (Aug., 2002), pp. 297-305

[31] JRC. European Commission. 2011.The Consumer Empowerment Index

http://ec.europa.eu/consumers/consumer_empowerment/docs/JRC_report_consumer_empowerment_en.pdf

The Evolution Of Openness

Collaboration On Shared Platforms

Shane Coughlan
Founder
Opendawn
Japan
shane@opendawn.com

Abstract—Free Software is an approach to software that emphasises the freedoms provided to end users, with a particular focus on the ability of participants to use, study, share and improve technology. Its popularity has produced a wealth of related terminology and advocates, and this occasionally leads to some degree of confusion or misunderstanding. However, once Free Software is understood as a method of deriving value from knowledge products with an emphasis on collaboration, and as existing in a world where such activities tend to easier, cheaper and more effective than ever before, the reason for both its popularity and growth becomes clear. This paper asserts that Free Software will continue to benefit from and drive increased openness and interoperability in the technology market. Perhaps most interestingly, as the concepts underlying Free Software are applied to other creative works such as text, music or images, mainstream acceptance of this approach to developing and maintaining knowledge products will increase. The governance of such approaches - and therefore their sustainability - will be refined as they scale, and any issues will gradually be worked out due to stakeholder requirements and market dynamics.

I. Defining And Understanding Free Software

Free and Open Source Software (Free Software) is an approach to software that facilitates multiple development and business models. It is best characterised as a software paradigm. A software paradigm (also referred to as a software model) helps contextualise how stakeholders will create, distribute and/or use the software on computers. There are different software paradigms that compete for attention, investment and market-share in the modern business environment. The two predominant software paradigms are termed proprietary and Free Software, with the criteria for differentiation being based on the level of control over software that each facilitates. With proprietary software, control tends to lie primarily with the vendor, while with Free Software control tends to be weighted towards the end user.

II. The Origin Of Free Software

Free Software originated in the USA during the early 1980s. While in the early years of computer science it was common for people to share software, the concept of selling software had begun to change this practice. What is termed the 'Software Industry' started in the early 1960s, and by the late 1970s it had grown significantly, due in no small part to the development of the personal computer in the mid-1970s and the rise of companies such as Microsoft.[1] The tension between those who wanted to share software technology and those who wanted to charge for access to software is best exemplified by a letter Bill Gates wrote to the Homebrew Computer Club in 1976.[2] Entitled 'An Open Letter to Hobbyists', it charged that the practice of sharing code damaged the ability of people to produce good software.[3]

In 1983 Richard Stallman, an employee at MIT's Artificial Intelligence laboratory, decided to formalise the concepts behind the sharing of software technology. He founded a project to create a complete Free Software operating system that was compatible with Unix called the GNU Project.[4] This also necessitated the development of terminology to describe how and why the Free Software paradigm worked.[5] In 1985 this emerging 'Free Software Movement' consolidated with Mr Stallman's establishment of the Free Software Foundation, the formal publisher and maintainer of the first and the most popular Free Software licences.[6]

III. The definition of Free Software

Free Software is not simply an aspiration to share software. It is a formally defined set of attributes applied to compliant software. The first formal definition of Free Software is hosted on the GNU Project website.[7] A concise overview is provided by Richard Stallman in his 2002 book, 'Free Software, Free Society':

"The term "Free Software" is sometimes misunderstood—it has nothing to do with price. It is about freedom. Here, therefore, is the definition of Free Software: a program is Free Software, for you, a particular user, if:
• You have the freedom to run the program, for any purpose.

---

1   http://en.wikipedia.org/wiki/Software_industry
2   http://en.wikipedia.org/wiki/Open_Letter_to_Hobbyists
3   Ibid.
4   http://www.gnu.org/
5   http://en.wikipedia.org/wiki/Free_software
6   http://www.fsf.org/
7   http://www.gnu.org/philosophy/free-sw.html

• You have the freedom to modify the program to suit your needs. (To make this

freedom effective in practice, you must have access to the source code, since

making changes in a program without having the source code is exceedingly

difficult.)

• You have the freedom to redistribute copies, either gratis or for a fee.

• You have the freedom to distribute modified versions of the program, so that

the community can benefit from your improvements." [8]

These four freedoms have been simplified in certain ways to illustrated the benefits of the approach. On the front page of the GNU Project website it suggests that "To understand the concept, you should think of "free" as in "free speech", not as in "free beer"."[9] Another is to shorten the four freedoms themselves into the form of 'use, study, share and improve.'[10]

IV. FREE SOFTWARE IS NOT COMMUNISM

In 2000, Steve Ballmer, Chief Executive Office of Microsoft, famously likened Free Software to Communism.[11] However, its advocates have never positioned it as such, and would point out that it is not and has never been a movement against the principles of financial gain nor is it inherently anti-corporate. Rather the opposite, in the sense that Free Software explicitly and purposefully allows commercial exploitation.[12]

This being said, Richard Stallman contends that key stakeholders in early software production were acting a way that he found unethical. He felt they were abusing their position and by doing so abusing the users of computers. It could be suggested that this was less of an anti-market stance than an observation regarding inefficiency and control given, of course, that we assume markets are intended to serve the majority participating rather than a narrow group who control supply and demand:

"The modern computers of the era, such as the VAX or the 68020, had their own operating systems, but none of them were Free Software: you had to sign a non-disclosure agreement even to get an executable copy.

This meant that the first step in using a computer was to promise not to help your neighbour. A cooperating community was forbidden. The rule made by the owners of proprietary software was, "If you share with your neighbour, you are a pirate. If you want any changes, beg us to make them."

The idea that the proprietary-software social system—the system that says you are not allowed to share or change software—is antisocial, that it is unethical, that it is simply wrong, may come as a surprise to some readers. But what else could we say about a system based on dividing the public and keeping users helpless? Readers who find the idea surprising may have taken this proprietary-software social system as given, or judged it on the terms suggested by proprietary software businesses. Software publishers have worked long and hard to convince people that there is only one way to look at the issue." [13]

Stallman's issue could be described as what people now may term 'lock-in' and 'market distortion.' His perspective has since been validated in two critical ways, one being the recent spate of anti-trust cases and the other being the wholesale commercial adoption of Free Software precisely because it facilitates

competition, market growth and the maximisation of investment.

V. FREE SOFTWARE IS NOT EXTREMISM

Those involved in Free Software did not perceive it to be an extreme movement. They did perceive it to be different to what a relatively narrow set of self-interested parties wished, but that's a different matter. Professor Laurence Lessig sums it up well with his introduction to 'Free Software, Free Society':

"there are those who call Stallman's message too extreme. But extreme it is not. Indeed, in an obvious sense, Stallman's work is a simple translation of the freedoms that our tradition crafted in the world before code. "Free Software" would assure that the world governed by code is as "free" as our tradition that built the world before code." [14]

VI. WHERE DID ALL THE DOUBT COME FROM?

It is reasonable to suggest that there were a narrow set of parties with vested interests who were extremely worried about Free Software, and expended a lot of money and time trying to undermine it. The reason is that Free Software as a paradigm presents a significant challenge to proprietary software as a paradigm. Proprietary software depends on charging per-copy licence fees to derive the majority of its profit. Free Software imposes no per-copy licence fees.

VII. FREE SOFTWARE WORKS

However, those working to challenge Free Software's credibility ultimately failed for a very simple reason. Free Software is an approach to software that allows people to do a great deal with code..Some people (usually computer scientists like Richard Stallman) understood that Free Software was a good idea in its early days. Some people (perhaps those from portfolio management or sales backgrounds) took longer to understand the benefit. Nowadays all types of parties in all types of segments see value in Free Software.

---

8   http://www.gnu.org/philosophy/fsfs/rms-essays.pdf (page 26)
9   http://www.gnu.org/
10 http://lwn.net/Articles/308594/
11 http://www.theregister.co.uk/2000/07/31/ms_ballmer_linux_is_communism/
12 http://www.fsf.org/licensing/essays/selling.html

13 http://www.gnu.org/philosophy/fsfs/rms-essays.pdf, page 24.
14 http://www.gnu.org/philosophy/fsfs/rms-essays.pdf, page 18.

VIII. Practical use of Free Software is framed by licences

The goals of Free Software are realised through licences governed by copyright law. These licences tend to take an unusual form compared to traditional proprietary documents. Instead of providing a narrow grant of use with a long list of exceptions and restrictions, Free Software licences tend to provide a broad grant of use with few restrictions. These licences are often divided into three categories; non-Copyleft, weak-Copyleft and strong-Copyleft.

IX. Copyleft is a mechanism used to preserve Free Software

Richard Stallman wanted to ensure that the primary project in Free Software, the GNU Operating System, would be available to people with the four freedoms he had identified as being important, and he wanted to ensure this availability would continue in the mid-to-long-term. To do this he formulated Copyleft.

"The goal of GNU was to give users freedom, not just to be popular. So we needed to use distribution terms that would prevent GNU software from being turned into proprietary software. The method we use is called copyleft.

Copyleft uses copyright law, but flips it over to serve the opposite of its usual purpose: instead of a means of privatizing software, it becomes a means of keeping software free." [15]

Copyleft says that the freedoms provided with the software apply to all subsequent users of the software as well. Copyleft is not an inherent characteristic of Free Software, but rather a way of maintaining a set of grants applied to the software in question. This is a distinction sometimes overlooked by people new to Free Software, leading to confusion when encountering Free Software licences that provide the ability to use, study, share and improve code according to the formal definition of the Free Software Foundation, yet not containing Copyleft provisions.

X. Understanding what type of licence is important

A very common question during early use of Free Software centres around which type of Free Software licence is important or beneficial, non-Copyleft, weak-Copyleft and strong-Copyleft. Some would suggest that non-Copyleft licences are best because the cooperative model does not require formal statements of subsequent sharing.[16] Some maintain that they want an explicit Copyleft requirement applied to their code.[17] Some parties like the Free Software Foundation advocate the use of strong-Copyleft whenever possible.[18]

The form of licence is used by over 50% of Free Software are strong-Copyleft licences such as the GNU GPL.[19] It is most notably used on the Linux kernel,[20] most of the GNU Project,[21] and other critical technologies like SAMBA.[22] This is probably because strong-Copyleft provides a very predictable and stable grant for the technology, allowing multiple parties to cooperate in using and developing it over prolonged periods.

XI. Controversy regarding the politics of the GPL

The GNU GPL was created to enshrine the four freedoms and the principle of Copyleft in a legal document. It is a strong-Copyleft Free Software licence. Its purpose has never been otherwise, as Stallman's description of its origin attests:

"The specific implementation of copyleft that we use for most GNU software is the GNU General Public License, or GNU GPL for short." [23]

The GNU GPL is a very popular Free Software licence, accounting for over half of the total Free Software licence use according to Black Duck research.[24] The most widely used variant of the GPL is version 2 of the licence, though version 3 – released in 2007 – is becoming increasingly popular and has been adopted by major code projects like SAMBA.[25]

Some parties may in the past have become indignant that the GPL contains a preamble that explains its originals and purpose, and that this makes it a political manifesto as well as a legal document.[26] Alternatively it could be argued that the preamble serves a useful purpose in explaining the purpose and intended scope of the following license, as evidenced by - for instance – its first paragraph in version two of the licence:

"The licenses for most software are designed to take away your freedom to share and change it. By contrast, the GNU General Public License is intended to guarantee your freedom to share and change Free Software--to make sure the software is free for all its users. This General Public License applies to most of the Free Software Foundation's software and to any other program whose authors commit to using it. (Some other Free Software Foundation software is covered by the GNU Lesser General Public License instead.) You can apply it to your programs, too."[27]

While there is little doubt that organisations such as the Free Software Foundation have a political agenda, Free Software licences such as the GPL are no more valid or invalid because of this then the licences of a traditional software company are rendered valid or invalid due to the company having a financial interest in the market.

---

15 http://www.gnu.org/philosophy/fsfs/rms-essays.pdf, page 28.
16 http://www.onlamp.com/pub/a/onlamp/2005/06/30/esr_interview.html
17 http://www.freesoftwaremagazine.com/columns/why_i_choose_copyleft_for_my_projects
18 http://www.fsf.org/licensing/licenses/why-not-lgpl.html
19 http://www.blackducksoftware.com/oss
20 http://en.wikipedia.org/wiki/Linux
21 http://en.wikipedia.org/wiki/GNU
22 http://us6.samba.org/samba/docs/GPL.html
23 http://www.gnu.org/philosophy/fsfs/rms-essays.pdf, page 29.
24 http://www.blackducksoftware.com/oss
25 http://news.samba.org/announcements/samba_gplv3/
26 http://www.netc.org/openoptions/background/history.html
27 http://www.gnu.org/licenses/gpl-2.0.html

XII. Controversy Regarding the Validity of the GPL

As Free Software grew into a mainstream approach in IT, questions were raised about whether the primary licence used, the GNU GPL, was actually valid.[28] These questions suggested that the model applied by Free Software was not something that worked in copyright law, and were initially contested by essays produced by figures central to the Free Software Movement.[29] Later they were contested more substantially through court cases against parties infringing the GPL licence in Europe.[30] These cases resulted in court victories, and were followed by events in the USA that further validated the licensing approach[31] and its effectiveness in being applied to commercial transactions.[32]

Today there is little doubt the GPL is a valid legal document. Version 2 is well-entrenched in the market, and the growing use of version 3 has occurred despite some criticism of the document while it was being drafted.[33] This may be indicative that such criticism, as with criticism directed at earlier versions of the GPL or at Free Software itself, was largely unfounded. It is also possible to suggest that criticism of the GPL provoked responses, elaboration and clarification that contributed to maturing the licence, and perhaps the paradigm as a whole.

XIII. A World Where People Can Work Together

The Internet has allowed people to communicate and to work together across great distances at a lower cost and at a higher speed than ever before. It has been a powerful driver in reducing barriers to working with partners and customers to accomplish goals, what is sometimes referred to as co-innovation.[34] In the software field it is difficult for a single vendor to meet all the requirements of multiple customers, and it is more effective for several parties to cooperate on developing and enhancing a shared platform. This is what increasingly happens, and it has lead to the commercial sustainability of Free Software projects such as the Linux kernel.[35] This is because Free Software, a software paradigm build on the inherent assumption of cooperation and sharing, is a natural beneficiary of trends towards cooperation.

---

28 See for example Andrés Guadamuz (2004) 'Viral Contracts or Unenforceable Documents? Contractual Validity of Copyleft Licenses', E.I.P.R. Vol. 26, Issue 8, pp.331-339. Also online at http://papers.ssrn.com/sol3/papers.cfm?abstract_id=569101
29 http://www.gnu.org/philosophy/enforcing-gpl.html
30 http://gpl-violations.org/news/20040519-iptables-sitecom.html
31 http://www.fsf.org/news/wallace-vs-fsf
32 http://www.softwarefreedom.org/news/2007/oct/30/busybox-monsoon-settlement/
33 http://www.eweek.com/c/a/Linux-and-Open-Source/Latest-Draft-of-GPL-3-Comes-Under-Fire/
34 http://theotherthomasotter.wordpress.com/2007/05/03/co-innovation-is-a-strength-not-a-weakness/
35 http://linuxfoundation.org/en/Members

XIV. Working Together Case-Study: The Linux Kernel

The Linux kernel started as a student project,[36] and has grown into the core of an operating system used in a wide variety of fields with financial backing from companies like Fujitsu, Hitachi, HP, IBM, Intel, NEC, Novell, and Oracle.[37] Linux is GPL software designed to run on many types of computer, and it is developed through a world-wide cooperative project on the Internet.[38] Given its scale and success, it provides an excellent example of co-innovative development inside the Free Software paradigm. It is structured into teams with leaders who consolidate work, and a handful of key developers that then combine the components into the final product. There is a relatively low barrier to entry regarding participation in development, and each individual stakeholder will have their own reasons for investing in the project. What is noticeable is that the collective output of the parties collaborating is stable, reliable and widely used in critical industries.

XV. Cooperation Changes How We Work

Cooperation in creating software has profound implications for development models and the management of processes. It requires the broad sharing of information and tools without delay between multiple parties and even legal entities, with an emphasis on reducing access time further to optimise the benefit of cooperation. In the last few years an increasing number of formal models have been emerging to facilitate this, with one example being 'Agile software development,' which places emphasis on the feedback provided by creative participants to guide further development.[39]

XVI. Cooperation Is Here To Stay

Cooperative development is arguable permanent for two reasons, one systemic and one market-based. From the systemic perspective, the reduction of barriers and costs to cooperation have lead to a self-sustaining cycle where new development models have emerged that increase the efficiency of cooperation, and in turn foster further optimisation and investment in the activity. From a market perspective, users are requiring more complex and interconnected software, and without unlimited engineering resources the most efficient way to produce such software is through building shared, interoperable platforms with other market participants.

XVII. Increased User Involvement

---

36 http://www.linux.org/people/linus_post.html
37 http://linuxfoundation.org/en/FAQ#Who_are_members_of_the_Linux_Foundation.3F
38 http://www.kernel.org/
39 http://en.wikipedia.org/wiki/Agile_software_development

Cooperation does not mean working with a small, select group of similar companies. That is a template for cooperation somewhat tied to the Industrial Revolution, and rather less applicable to a world where instant communication allows an individual in Shenyang, China to work as effectively as a cubicle worker in London.

The dynamics of the software industry have altered in the last two decades. Twenty years ago the dominant proprietary paradigm resulted in a small number of providers controlling innovation and serving a large number of users in a fairly static relationship. However, the emerging Free Software paradigm encouraged new development models and new software development processes that moved the decision-making emphasis to users. Since the Free Software paradigm gained mainstream traction this has had a profound effect on the market as a whole. Increased user involvement in consultation, design, testing and improvement is noticeable in every approach to software today. One result of these developments has been to blur the distinction between what constitutes a user and what constitutes a provider. Free Software notably empowers all users to become providers at any time of their choosing.

XVIII. THERE ARE MANY DEVELOPMENT MODELS IN FREE SOFTWARE

The proprietary software and Free Software paradigms facilitate the establishment and improvement of various software development models and processes. These development models may be hierarchical, loosely managed or unstructured depending on the given software paradigm and the requirements of the individuals or organisations working on a project. It would be incorrect to attempt to associate Free Software exclusively with one development or business model, though such an approach has in the past been unfortunately common.

Such misconceptions are partly attributable to an essay by Eric Raymond circulated in 1997 entitled "The Cathedral and the Bazaar,"[40] and extended into a book published by O'Reilly Media in 1999.[41] The proposition that "given enough eyeballs, all bugs are shallow" appeared to suggest that the limited, hierarchical and restricted world of proprietary commercial software ultimately could not compete with the broad, dynamic and more bazaar-like world of Free Software. However, it should be understood that Mr. Raymond's paper was not originally a comparison of the Free Software development methodology versus a proprietary development methodology. It was a criticism of hierarchical structures applied by the GNU Project (a Free Software project) versus the more flat management structure of the Linux Project (a Free Software project).[42]

XIX. QUESTIONING FREE SOFTWARE IN A COMMERCIAL WORLD

Some people have difficulty understanding the approach taken with Free Software, and have questioned its validity as a commercial approach.[43] However, concern with regards viable business models and Free Software tends to arise when parties have a preconception that per-unit licence costs are inherent to commercial software. While Free Software allows a wealth of business models to be applied, per-unit licensing costs is not one of them.

Per-unit revenue models would either have to prevent sharing of code to maximise their market and thus undermine one of the four freedoms defined by the Free Software Foundation, or they would be circumvented by users who would have a choice of paying the originator for a copy of the software or getting one from a third-party without cost.

XX. BUSINESS MODELS IN FREE SOFTWARE

There are many business models applicable to Free Software. This is for the same reason that Free Software facilitates multiple development models; as a paradigm Free Software draws a wide set of parameters that participants operate inside.

The most common Free Software business models in the server and workstation market segment tend to be support provision across multiple products (al la IBM)[44] or support provision for a branded family of products (al la Red Hat).[45] Embedded companies (those that make telephones, routers and other small computing devices) now frequently make use of Free Software. The business models applied tend towards mixed-model, with a Free Software platform being used to provide basic services, and perhaps a proprietary series of components to provide a differentiator. MontaVista's products in the embedded networking sphere provide an example of this.[46]

In network services there are many companies using Free Software. Most notable is Google, which uses Free Software-based technologies to power its infrastructure, and makes a modified Free Software operating system available for its employees workstations.[47] Because Google provides network services exclusively, rather than through the distribution of software, the use of Free Software has very little impact on their business model except to reduce costs, and their modifications to Free Software code do not have to be distributed. This has come under some criticism as effectively using Free Software without fully participating in the paradigm.[48] However, regardless of what one thinks of their use of the code, Google's business model has proven highly successful. In essence, they used Free Software to facilitate

---

40 http://www.catb.org/~esr/writings/cathedral-bazaar/
41 http://oreilly.com/catalog/9780596001315/
42 http://www.alamut.com/subj/economics/misc/cathedral.html

43 http://business.timesonline.co.uk/tol/business/industry_sectors/technology/article733264.ece
44 http://www-03.ibm.com/linux/
45 http://www.redhat.com/
46 http://www.mvista.com/
47 http://en.wikipedia.org/wiki/Google_platform
48 http://ostatic.com/blog/google-touts-open-source-cred

infrastructure that would have cost billions to build as proprietary software, and they leveraged this to provide services.

XXI. FINDING THE FREE SOFTWARE BUSINESS MODEL

Ultimately the number of possible business models applicable to Free Software make it impossible to pick out any one as a clear favourite. As with any field of business, the correct model depends on market segment analysis, an understanding of your skills, and a prudent balance between maximisation of profit and sustainability. There is no 'Free Software business model' in the singular sense; the licences provide broad grants that foster a wide range of activities.

XXII. FREE SOFTWARE WILL CONTINUE TO GROW

Research by Gartner suggests that 85% of enterprises are already using Free Software in one capacity or another, and the remaining 15% expect to use it within twelve months.[49] These figures the type of market penetration figures previously suggested by UNU Merit, when in their 2007 report for the European Commission they suggested that "FLOSS-related services could reach a 32% share of all IT services by 2010, and the FLOSS-related share of the economy could reach 4% of European GDP by 2010."[50] There is no indication that the growth of Free Software will slow at any point in the near future, given fair market access.

XXIII. THE MODERN SOFTWARE MARKET REQUIRES OPENNESS AND INTEROPERABILITY

It is important that fair and equitable competition is fostered in markets regardless of the software paradigm chosen by participants. Competition drives innovation and provides an impartial method of determining the success or failure of products, businesses and approaches. Given this, access to information regarding interoperability and interaction between software components is a key requirement in the modern IT market. Conversely, if fair access is not provided, then competitive paradigms like Free Software may be hindered in terms of future market penetration.

XXIV. FREE SOFTWARE AND STANDARDISATION

Free Software and standardisation is an area that has been drawing increasing interest. This is best exemplified by the public debate over what became known as MS-OOXML, a next generation document format. It was suggested that the process was biased[51] and that the grants provided for the proposed standard were insufficient for Free Software.[52]

A great deal of the discussion surrounding standardisation and Free Software centred on patents. The reason for this are the are fundamentally different goals for patents and standards, as illustrated by Mr Karsten Meinhold, chairman of the ETSI IPR Special Committee, when he stated that "IPRs and Standards serve different purposes: IPRs are destined for private exclusive use, standards are intended for public, collective use."[53] Free Software, being also designed for public, collective use, tends not to fall into the normal categorisation of how IPR is positioned.

Patents in standards had previously been managed by grants such as RAND, and these were considered sufficient for proprietary software. However, that did not mean that such conditions facilitated fair market access and competition for all software paradigms competing in the market. For example, per-unit royalty payments would compromise the freedom of people to share the code, as would terms that did not permit sub-licensing.

Indeed, several Free Software licences have provisions regarding issues like patents to ensure that the four freedoms defined by the copyright licence continue in full to all subsequent users. The GPL is an example of such a licence, and others with the same or similar provisions actually make up the majority of the Free Software paradigm. For example, according to Black Duck research 66.57% of projects use GPL family licences that explicitly prohibit the application of patent restrictions on covered software.[54] Excluding these licences from a standard would mean excluding 2/3 of the Free Software model participants from accessing that standard.

XXV. GLOBALIZATION AND FREE SOFTWARE

Ultimately the success of Free Software may be a product of Globalisation. Globalisation refers to the process of national economies becoming more open, economics becoming more 'global' than 'national', and to the reduction of national controls over economic matters.[55] In effect, changing the world from a loose organisation of states into a single giant canvas. In doing so, it provides new opportunities for people to work together.

This proposition is contested by 'globalisation scepticism', a view summed up by Hirst and Thompson's comment that "the closer we looked the shallower and more unfounded became the claims of the more radical advocates of economic globalization".[56] For these sceptics there are international economies but there is no evidence for a truly 'global'

---

49 http://www.gartner.com/it/page.jsp?id=801412
50 http://flossimpact.eu/
51 http://www.linuxjournal.com/node/1000294
52 http://arstechnica.com/software/news/2008/03/sflc-ooxml-could-poses-patent-threat-to-gpl-licensed-software.ars
53 http://ec.europa.eu/enterprise/ict/policy/standards/ws08ipr/presentations/21meinhold_en.pdf
54 http://www.blackducksoftware.com/oss
55 Ramesh Mishra, Globalization and the Welfare State, (Cheltenham: Edward Elgar, 1999), 3-4.
56 Paul Hirst and Grahame Thompson, Globalization in Question: The International Economy and the Possibilities, 2nd ed. (Cambridge: Polity Press, 1999), p2.

economy.[57] A valid criticism, but relevant only in the context of purely economic, rather than cultural or communicative Globalisation.

Whether one defines Globalisation as an example of increasing global capitalism or as a deeper and more complex mix of political, cultural and financial connections, it suggests that the world is not merely a collection of states with limited communication and sharing potential.

From the perspective of technology and business, it does not matter whether globalisation is a trend towards a global economy or a collection of increasingly interlinked international economies. Knowledge, goods and people are far more mobile now than ever before. Software, a technology that can be easily transferred through communication networks, is perhaps the greatest beneficiary of this development.

XXVI. Free Software has spread beyond software

The concept beyond Free Software have proven to be influential beyond the sphere of code production and beyond even the field of technology. The most important recent example is that Professor Laurence Lessig applied the concepts behind Free Software to the sharing of other creative work, and formed what is now known as the Creative Commons. In the introduction to Lessig's primary book on cultural sharing, 'Free Culture,' he states:

"The inspiration for the title and for much of the argument of this book comes from the work of Richard Stallman and the Free Software Foundation. Indeed, as I reread Stallman's own work, especially the essays in Free Software, Free Society, I realize that all of the theoretical insights I develop here are insights Stallman described decades ago."[58]

XXVII. Conclusion

Free Software is an approach to software that emphasises the freedoms provided to end users, with a particular focus on the ability of participants to use, study, share and improve technology. While occasionally misunderstood as being non-commercial, Free Software has always been conceptualised as something that allows commercial activity. It is framed by its licences, which range from providing a simple, non-perpetual grant of the receiving user freedom (as with the Modified BSD licence) through to providing such freedom in perpetuity via Copyleft and addressing issues such as patents (as with the GPL). While still relatively new, most concerns related to this approach to licensing have been substantially addressed in courts of law, in industry usage and in common understanding over the licence terms and their intent. Today Free Software has become a central component of mainstream IT.

The popularity of Free Software has produced a wealth of related terminology and perspectives, and this occasionally leads to some degree of confusion or misunderstanding. To address this it is necessary to go back to first principles in defining Free Software, understanding the concept of licensing that underpins it, and examining how it facilitates multiple development and business models. This leads to a number of useful observations. The first is that Free Software is a paradigm that facilitates a multitude of development and business models, barring only those inherently tied to the concept of per-unit software licence fees. The second is that Free Software benefits from globalisation, especially in the context of increasing long-distance cooperation facilitated by the Internet. This applies equally whether one is concerned with cooperation between like-minded professionals or with blurring the distinction between a developer and a user of technology.

Once Free Software is understood as a method of deriving value from knowledge products with an emphasis on collaboration, it naturally follows that its productive application depends on good governance and active collaboration. It is well positioned because it facilitates sharing and cooperation in a world where such activities tend to easier, cheaper and more effective than ever before. It is therefore reasonable to assert that Free Software will continue to benefit from and drive increased openness and interoperability in the technology market for pragmatic reasons.

In conclusion, as the concepts underlying Free Software are applied to other creative works such as text, music or images, mainstream acceptance of this approach to developing and maintaining knowledge products will increase. Its governance - and therefore sustainability - will be refined as it scales, and any issues will gradually be worked out due to stakeholder requirements and market dynamics.

---

57 Ibid, p16.
58 http://www.free-culture.cc/freecontent/, page 14.

Open Content Mining

Peter Murray-Rust
University of Cambridge and OKFN
Cambridge, UK
pm286@cam.ac.uk

Jennifer C Molloy
University of Oxford and OKFN
Oxford, UK
jenny.molloy@okfn.org

Diane Cabell
Oxford e-Research Centre, Creative Commons and iCommons Ltd.
Oxford, UK
dc@icommons.org

Abstract— We present evidence that content-mining of scholarly articles is now technically feasible and highly valuable both. However researchers and information technologist are blocked by legal and contractual barries from using it and developing the methodologies. We review the problems and propose changes in legal policy which we have already submitted to the UK's Hargreaves report on intellectual property reform. We put forward the fundamental rights of scholars and embed them in a manifesto: "The right to read is the right to mine", "Users and providers should encourage machine processing, and "Facts don't belong to anyone".

Index Terms—Open Knowledge, Content mining, Hargreaves process, Text mining, publishers, legal barriers

I. Introduction

As scientists and scholars, we are both creators and users of information. Our work, however, only achieves its full value when it is shared with other researchers so as to forward the progress of science. One's data becomes exponentially more useful when combined with the data of others. Today's technology provides an unprecedented capacity for such data combination.

Researchers can now find and read papers online, rather than having to manually track down print copies. Machines (computers) can index the papers and extract the details (titles, keywords etc.) in order to alert scientists to relevant material. In addition, computers can extract factual data and meaning by "mining" the content.

We illustrate the technology and importance of content-mining with 3 graphical examples which represent the state of the art today (Fig.1-3). These are all highly scalable (i.e. can be applied to thousands or even millions of target papers without human intervention. There are unavoidable errors for unusual documents and content and there is a trade-off between precision ("accuracy") and recall ("amount retrieved") but in many cases we and others have achieved 95% precision. The techniques are general for scholarly publications and can be applied to theses, patents and formal reports as well as articles in peer-reviewed journals.

A:

To a solution of 3-bromobenzophenone (1.00 g, 4 mmol) in MeOH (15 mL) was added sodium borohydride (0.3 mL, 8 mmol) portionwise at rt and the suspension was stirred at rt for 1-24 h. The reaction was diluted slowly with water and extracted with CH2Cl2. The organic layer was washed successively with water, brine, dried over Na2SO4, and concentrated to give the title compound as oil (0.8 g, 79%), which was used in the next reaction without further purification. MS (ESI, pos. ion) m/z: 247.1 (M-OH).

B:

C:

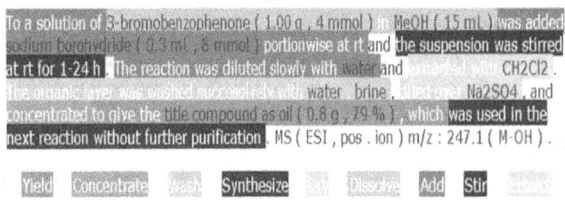

Fig. 1. "Text mining". (a) the raw text as published in a scientific journal, thesis or patent. (b) Entity recognition (the compounds in the text are identified) and shallow parsing to extract the sentence structure and heuristic identification of the roles of phrases (c) complete analysis of the chemical reaction by applying heuristics to the result of (b). We have analyzed about half a million chemical reactions in US patents (with Lezan Hawizy and Daniel Lowe).

Content mining is the way that modern technology makes use of digital information. Because the scientific community is now globally connected, digitized information is being uploaded from hundreds of thousands of different sources [1]. With current data sets measuring in terabytes [2], it is often no longer possible to simply read a scholarly summary in order to make scientifically significant use of such information [3]. A researcher must be able to copy information, recombine it with other data and otherwise "re-use" it to produce truly helpful results. Not only is mining a deductive tool to analyze research data, it is the very mechanism by which search engines operate to allow discovery of content, making connections – and even scientific discoveries – that might otherwise remain invisible to researchers. To prevent mining would force scientists into blind alleys and silos where only limited knowledge is accessible. Science does not progress if it cannot incorporate the most recent findings to move forward.

However, use of this exponentially liberating research process is blocked both by publisher-imposed restraints and by law. These constraints are based on business models that still rely on print revenue and are supported by copyright laws originally designed for 18th century stationers [4]. While Open Access (OA) practices are improving the ability of researchers to read papers (by removing access barriers), still only around 20% of scholarly papers are offered under OA terms [5]. The remainder are locked behind pay walls. As per the terms imposed by the vast majority of journal subscription contracts, subscribers may read pay-walled papers but they may not mine them.

Securing permission to mine on a journal-by-journal basis is extraordinarily time consuming. According to the Wellcome Trust, 87% of the material housed in UK's main medical research database (UK PubMedCentral) is unavailable for legal text and data mining [6]. A recent study funded by the Joint Information Systems Committee (JISC), an association funded by UK higher education institutions, frames the scale of the problem:

In the free-to-access, UKPMC repository there are 2930 full-text articles, published since 2000, which have the word 'malaria' in the title.

Of these 1,818 (62%) are Open Access and thus suitable for text mining without having to seek permission. However, the remaining 1,112 articles (38%) are not open access, and thus permission from the rights-holder to text-mine this content must be sought.

The 1,112 articles were published in 187 different journals, published by 75 publishers.

As publisher details are not held in the UKPMC database, the permission-seeking researcher will need to make contact with every journal. Using a highly conservative estimate of one hour research per journal title (i.e., to find contact address, indicate which articles they wish to text-mine, send letters, follow-up non-responses, and record permissions etc.) this

A:
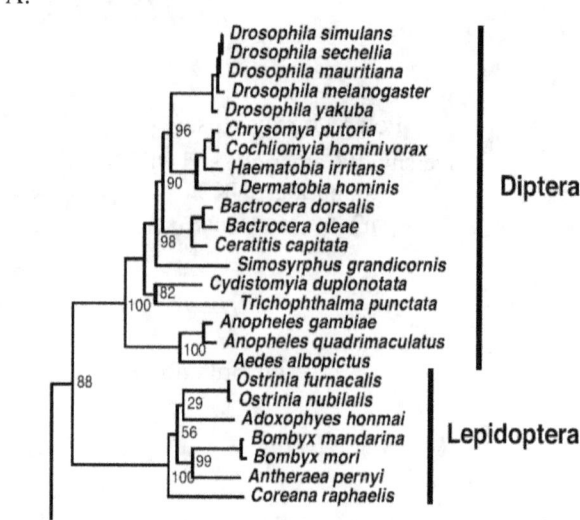

B:
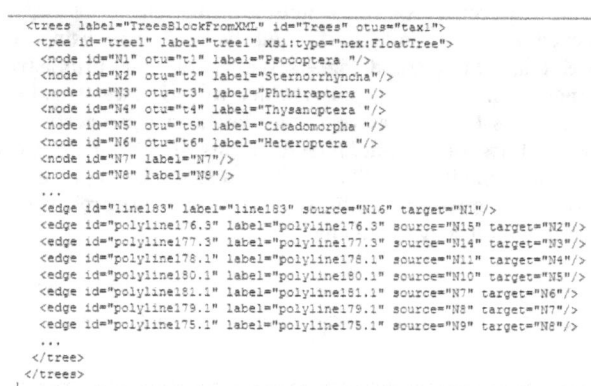

Fig. 2. Mining content in "full-text". (a) a typical "phylogenetic tree" [snippet] representing the similarity of species (taxa) – the horizontal scale can be roughly mapped onto an evolutionary timeline; number are confidence estimates and critical for high quality work. These trees are of great value in understanding speciation and biodiversity and may require thousands of hours of computation and are frequently only published as diagrams. (b) Extraction of formal content as domain-standard (NE)XML. This allows trees from different studies to be formally compared and potentially the creation of "supertrees" which can represent the phylogenetic relation of millions of species.

exercise will take 187 hours. Assuming that the researcher was newly qualified, earning around £30,000 pa, this single exercise would incur a cost of £3,399.

In reality however, a researcher would not limit his/her text mining analysis to articles which contained a relevant keyword in the title. Thus, if we expand this case study to find any full-text research article in UKPMC which mentions malaria (and published since 2000) the cohort increases from 2,930 to 15,757.

Of these, some 7,759 articles (49%), published in 1,024 journals, were not Open Access. Consequently, in this example, a researcher would need to contact 1,024 journals at a transaction cost (in terms of time spent) of £18,630; 62.1% of a working year .[7]

II. DATA AND THE LAW

The intention of copyright law is to support public dissemination of original works so that the public may benefit from access to them. It accomplishes this goal by granting to authors and creators a period of monopoly control over public use of their works so that they might maximize any market benefits. While these principles may work well to protect film producers and musicians, in the current digital environment it is the unfortunate case that they actually delay or block the effective re-use of research results by the scientific community. Research scientists rarely receive any share of the profits on sales of their journal articles, but do benefit greatly by having other scientists read and cite their work. Their interest is therefore best served by maximizing user access and use of their published results.

Databases are protected in a number of ways, most commonly by copyright and database laws. Copyright protects "creative expression" meaning the unique way that an author presents his intellectual output and it prohibits any one from copying, publicly distributing, and adapting the original without permission of the author. Specific statements of facts, shorn of any creative expression as is the case with many types of data, are themselves not ordinarily copyrightable as individual items. However, copyright does come into play for individual data points that exhibit creative expression, such as images (photographs). A collection of data can also be protected by copyright if there is sufficient creativity involved in the presentation or arrangement of the set. In the case of collections, it is only the right to utilize the collection as a whole that is restricted while the individual facts within the collection remain free.

Databases are additionally and independently protected under a *sui generis* regime imposed by the 1996 EU Database Directive [8]. Under the Directive, rights are granted to the one who makes a substantial investment in obtaining, verifying or presenting the contents of the database. Permission of the maker is required to extract or re-utilize all or a substantial portion of the database or to continuously extract or re-utilize insubstantial parts on a continuing basis.

To further complicate matters, copyright and database laws differ from each other and also from one jurisdiction to another. Copyrights may last for more than a hundred years (life of the author plus 70 years). Database rights (which could apply to the self-same database) only run for 15 years however those rights can be extended indefinitely by adding new data to produce a new "work" thus triggering a new term of rights, making it horrendously difficult to determine whether or not protection has expired. The United States, for example, does not impose any *sui generis* rights. Copyright ownership belongs to the creator or his employer, but may be transferred to another (such as a publisher) hence copyright ownership can be difficult to ascertain, particularly where multiple researchers have contributed to the whole. Legal rights in such cases may be jointly held and/or held by one or more employers and/or held by one or more publishers or repositories. The authors of many "orphan" works are unknown or unidentifiable. The more globally-developed the database, the more sets of laws come into play to further complicate the definition of rights.

A:

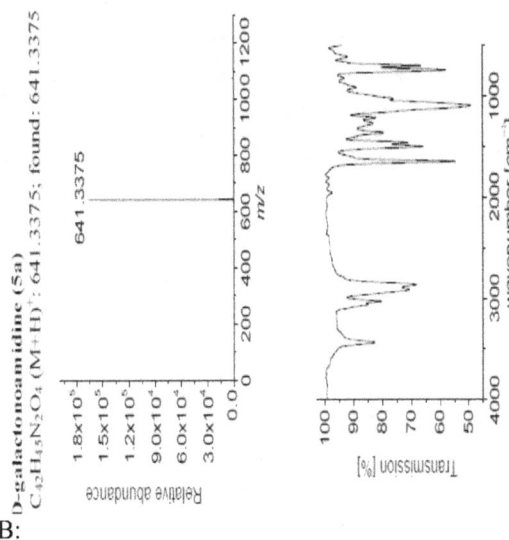

B:

Fig. 3. Content mining from "Supplemental Data" (or "Supporting Information"). This data is often deposited alongside the "full-text" of the journal, sometimes behind the publishers firewall, sometimes openly accessible. It may run to tens or hundreds of pages and for some scientists it is the most important part of the paper. (a) exactly as published [snippet]. Note the inconvenient orientation (designed for printing) and the apparent loss of detail. (b) after content mining techniques and re-orientation – for the "m/z" spectrum (note the fine structure of the main peak, not visible in (a)). It would be technically possible to recover >> 100,000 spectra like this per year from journals

There are exceptions to such laws when work may be used for specific purposes without permission of the owner. In the UK, these come under the rubric "fair dealing." The UK has a current exception for noncommercial research and private study, however much research is conducted by commercial entities such as pharmaceutical companies.

Even where the law would allow free use of data, publishers imposed restrictions (Table 1). The terms of the user's subscription contract – deemed to be a private contract by mutually consenting parties -- thus overrides any copyright or database freedoms allowed by law.

III. PROPOSED CHANGES IN LEGAL POLICY

Government studies have recognized the harm such restrictions cause to the advancement of science and economic development. They argue that mining is a "non-consumptive" use that does not directly trade on the underlying creative and

TABLE I. PUBLISHER CONTENT MINING POLICIES

Publisher	Table Column Head		
	License Agreement Link	Explicitly prohibits text/data mining?	Quote from standard license agreement
InformaWorld	http://www.informaworld.com/smpp/termsandconditions_partiiintellectualproperty	Yes	This licence does not include any derivative use of the Site or the Materials, any collection and use of any product listings, descriptions, or prices; any downloading or copying of account information for the benefit of another merchant; or any use of data mining, robots or similar data gathering and extraction tools. In addition, you may not use meta tags or any other "hidden text" utilising our name or the name of any of our group companies without our express written consent.
Taylor Francis	http://www.tandf.co.uk/journals/pdf/terms.pdf	Yes	Incorporates Informaworld terms – see above
Elsevier/CDL	http://orpheus-1.ucsd.edu/acq/license/cdlelsevier2004.pdf	Yes	"Schedule 1.2(a) General Terms and Conditions "RESTRICTIONS ON USAGE OF THE LICENSED PRODUCTS/ INTELLECTUAL PROPERTY RIGHTS" GTC1] "Subscriber shall not use spider or web-crawling or other software programs, routines, robots or other mechanized devices to continuously and automatically search and index any content accessed online under this Agreement. "
Blackwell	http://www.blackwellpublishing.com/pdf/Site_License.PDF	No	
OUP	http://www.oxfordjournals.org/help/instsitelicence.pdf	No	
Wiley	http://www.mpdl.mpg.de/nutzbed/wiley-interscience-backfile-co-nutzungsbedingung.pdf	Probably	The systematic downloading of data and the use of excerpts from databases for commercial purposes or for systematic distribution are prohibited.
ACS	http://www.mpdl.mpg.de/nutzbed/MPG_ACS_2002.pdf?la=en	Yes	Licensee (Consortium or Single Institution) acknowledges that ACS may prevent Members and their patrons, as the case may be, from using, implementing or authorizing use of any computerized or automated tool or application to search, index, test or otherwise obtain information from Licensed Materials (including without limitation any "spidering" or web crawler application) that has a detrimental impact on the use of the services under this Agreement.
AIP	http://www.mpdl.mpg.de/nutzbed/MPG_AIP.pdf	Yes	Systematic or programmatic downloading, printing, transmitting, or copying of the Licensed Materials is prohibited. "Systematic or Programmatic" means downloading, printing, transmitting, or copying activity of which the intent or the effect is to capture, reproduce, or transfer the entire output of a journal volume, a journal issue, or a journal topical section, or sequential or cumulative search results, or collections of abstracts, articles, tables of contents. Other such systematic or programmatic use of the Licensed Materials that interferes with the access of Authorized Users or that may affect the performance of SCITATION, for example, the use of "robots" to index content, or downloading or attempting to download large amounts of material in a short period of time, is prohibited. Redistribution of the Licensed Materials, except as permitted in Section 4, without permission of the Publishers and/or payment of a royalty to the Publishers or to the appropriate Reproduction Rights Organization, is prohibited
BMJ	http://group.bmj.com/group/about/legal/bmj-group-online-licence-single-institution-licence	No	
JSTOR	http://www.jstor.org/page/info/about/policies/terms.jsp	Yes	Prohibited Uses. Institutions and users may not:... f) undertake any activity that may burden JSTOR's server(s) such as computer programs that automatically download or export Content, commonly known as web robots, spiders, crawlers, wanderers or accelerators;
Nature	http://www.nature.com/libraries/site_licenses/2010acad_row.pdf	Yes	3. USAGE RESTRICTIONS Except as expressly permitted in Clause 2.1, the Licensee warrants that it will not, nor will it licence or permit others to, directly or indirectly, without the Licensor's prior written consent: (j) make mass, automated or systematic extractions from or hard copy storage of the Licenced Material.

expressive purpose of the original work or compete with its normal exploitation. Most recently, the 2011 Government-sponsored Hargreaves Report on intellectual property reform, found:

Researchers want to use every technological tool available, and they want to develop new ones. However, the law can block valuable new technologies, like text and data mining, simply because those technologies were not imagined when the law was formed. In teaching, the greatly expanded scope of what is possible is often unnecessarily limited by uncertainty about what is legal. Many university academics – along with teachers elsewhere in the education sector – are uncertain what copyright permits for themselves and their students. Administrators spend substantial sums of public money to entitle academics and research students to access works which have often been produced at public expense by academics and research students in the first place. Even where there are copyright exceptions established by law, administrators are often forced to prevent staff and students exercising them, because of restrictive contracts. Senior figures and institutions in the university sector have told the Review of the urgent need reform copyright to realise opportunities, and to make it clear what researchers and educators are allowed to do. [9]

Hargreaves recommended that the Government introduce a UK exception in the interim under the non-commercial research heading to allow use of analytics for non-commercial use, as in the malaria example above, as well as promoting at EU level an exception to support text mining and data analytics for commercial use. It argues that it is "not persuaded that restricting this transformative use of copyright material is necessary or in the UK's overall economic interest."[10]

Hargreaves also urged the government to change the law at both the national and EU level to prevent any copyright exceptions from being overridden by contract.

Applying contracts in that way means a rights holder can rewrite the limits the law has set on the extent of the right conferred by copyright. It creates the risk that should Government decide that UK law will permit private copying or text mining, these permissions could be denied by contract. Where an institution has different contracts with a number of providers, many of the contracts overriding exceptions in different areas, it becomes very difficult to give clear guidance to users on what they are permitted. Often the result will be that, for legal certainty, the institution will restrict access to the most restrictive set of terms, significantly reducing the provisions for use established by law. Even if unused, the possibility of contractual override is harmful because it replaces clarity ("I have the right to make a private copy") with uncertainty ("I must check my licence to confirm that I have the right to make a private copy"). The Government should change the law to make it clear no exception to copyright can be overridden by contract" [11]

The current U.K. government also believes that the ability for research to power economic development will be greatly enhanced if content mining is encouraged. In responding to Hargreaves, the Government stated its intention to:

- bring forward proposals for a substantial opening up of the UK's copyright exceptions regime, including a wide non-commercial research exception covering text and data mining, and
- aim to secure further flexibilities at EU level that enable greater adaptability to new technologies, and
- make the removal of EU level barriers to innovative and valuable technologies a priority to be pursued through all appropriate mechanisms. [12]

Further, the Government believes that it is not appropriate for "certain activities of public benefit such as medical research obtained through text mining to be in effect subject to veto by the owners of copyrights in the reports of such research, where access to the reports was obtained lawfully." [13]

Because science is a global enterprise, change in copyright law at the national and regional levels will not be sufficient to allow the free flow of information throughout the scientific community. Such changes must be made at many national and regional levels if the goal of a free and open exchange of data is to be achieved.

IV. CHANGES IN PUBLICATION POLICIES

Because publishers can override legal freedoms by enforcing restrictive terms of use in subscription agreements, we urge researchers to not only support these Government initiatives, but to go further by taking personal and institutional responsibility for establishing open mining practices in their work and publishing environments. In particular, we urge the adoption of the following Open Mining Manifesto [14].

V. OPEN MINING MANIFESTO

1) Define 'open content mining' in a broad and useful manner

'Open Content Mining' means the unrestricted right of subscribers to extract, process and republish content manually or by machine in whatever form (text, diagrams, images, data, audio, video, etc.) without prior specific permissions and subject only to community norms of responsible behaviour in the electronic age.

[1] Text
[2] Numbers
[3] Tables: numerical representations of a fact
[4] Diagrams (line drawings, graphs, spectra, networks, etc.): Graphical representations of relationships between variables, are images and therefore may not be, when considered as a collective entity, data. However, the individual data points underlying a graph, similar to tables, should be.
[5] Images and video (mainly photographic)- where it is the means of expressing a fact.
[6] Audio: same as images – where it expresses the factual representation of the research.

[7] XML: Extensible Markup Language (XML) defines rules for encoding documents in a format that is both human-readable and machine-readable."

[8] Core bibliographic data: described as "data which is necessary to identify and / or discover a publication" and defined under the Open Bibliography Principles [15].

[9] Resource Description Framework (RDF): information about content, such as authors, licensing information and the unique identifier for the article.

2) Urge publishers and institutional repositories to adhere to the following principles:

Principle 1: Right of Legitimate Accessors to Mine

We assert that there is no legal, ethical or moral reason to refuse to allow legitimate accessors of research content (OA or otherwise) to use machines to analyse the published output of the research community. Researchers expect to access and process the full content of the research literature with their computer programs and should be able to use their machines as they use their eyes. **The right to read is the right to mine**

Principle 2: Lightweight Processing Terms and Conditions

Mining by legitimate subscribers should not be prohibited by contractual or other legal barriers. Publishers should add clarifying language in subscription agreements that content is available for information mining by download or by remote access. Where access is through researcher-provided tools, no further cost should be required. **Users and providers should encourage machine processing**

Principle 3: Use

Researchers can and will publish facts and excerpts which they discover by reading and processing documents. They expect to disseminate and aggregate statistical results as facts and context text as fair use excerpts, openly and with no restrictions other than attribution. Publisher efforts to claim rights in the results of mining further retard the advancement of science by making those results less available to the research community; Such claims should be prohibited. **Facts don't belong to anyone.**

3. Strategies

Assert the above rights by:
- Educating researchers and librarians about the potential of content mining and the current impediments to doing so, including alerting librarians to the need not to cede any of the above rights when signing contracts with publishers
- Compiling a list of publishers and indicating what rights they currently permit, in order to highlight the gap between the rights here being asserted and what is currently possible
- Urging governments and funders to promote and aid the enjoyment of the above rights.

ACKNOWLEDGMENT

We thank Lezan Hawizy and Daniel Lowe for illustrations of text-mining and Ross Mounce for the phylogenetic trees.

REFERENCES

[1] McDonald, The Value and Benefits of Text Mining, Section 3.3.8, JISC Report Doc #811, March 2012, at http://www.jisc.ac.uk/publications/reports/2012/value-and-benefits-of-text-mining.aspx, citing P.J.Herron, "Text Mining Adoption for Pharmacogenomics-based Drug Discovery in a Large Pharmaceutical Company: a Case STudy," Library, 2006, claiming that text mining tools evaluated 50,000 patents in 18 months, a task that would have taken 50 person years to manually.

[2] Panzer-Steindel, Bernd, Sizing and Costing of the CERN T0 center, CERN-LCG-PEB-2004-21, 09 June 2004, at http://lcg.web.cern.ch/lcg/planning/phase2_resources/SizingandcostingoftheCERNT0center.pdf.

[3] See MEDLINE® Citation Counts by Year of Publication, at
http://www.nlm.nih.gov/bsd/medline_cit_counts_yr_pub.html and National Science Foundation, Science and Engineering Indicators: 2010, Chapter 5 at
http://www.nsf.gov/statistics/seind10/c5/c5h.htm
asserting the annual volume of scientific journal articles published is on the order of 2.5%.

[4] The Statute of Anne was the first UK law to provide for copyright regulation by government. See Statute of Anne, Wikipedia at http://en.wikipedia.org/wiki/Statute_of_Anne.

[5] Murray-Rust, The Right to Read is the Right to Mine, June 2012 at http://blog.okfn.org/2012/06/01/the-right-to-read-is-the-right-to-mine/.

[6] Hargreaves, Digital Opportunity, A Review of Intellectual Property and Growth, p. 47, May 2011, at http://www.ipo.gov.uk/ipreview-finalreport.pdf.

[7] McDonald, Value and benefits of text mining, March 2012, JISC at
http://www.jisc.ac.uk/publications/reports/2012/value-and-benefits-of-text-mining.aspxdata.

[8] Directive 96/9/EC of the European Parliament and of the Council of 11 March 1996 on the legal protection of

databases at
http://eur-lex.europa.eu/LexUriServ/LexUriServ.do?uri=CELEX:31996L0009:EN:HTML
and implemented in the UK by The Copyrights and Rights in Databases Regulations 1997 at http://www.legislation.gov.uk/uksi/1997/3032/contents/made.

[9] Hargreaves, supra, at p.41.

[10] Ibid., at p. 47.

[11] Ibid., at p. 51.

[12] The Government Response to the Hargreaves Review of Intellectual Property and Growth, p. 7 August 2011 at http://www.ipo.gov.uk/ipresponse-full.pdf.

[13] Ibid., Annex A at p.15.

[14] Murray-Rust, supra.

[15] Principles on Open Bibliographic Data at http://openbiblio.net/principles/

64

Complexities in the Relationship among Standarization, Invention and Innovation in Information and Communication Technologies

An introductory perspective

Jochen Friedrich
Technical Relations - Europe
IBM Germany
Mannheim, Germany
jochen@de.ibm.com

Abstract—Standards can play a key role for innovation, both regarding the exploitation of research results and inventions and regarding the promotion of innovation taking place on top the standards, on the level of the implementation. This paper gives an introductory outline on the various complexities around the relation of standardisation and innovation. It proposes a level of differentiation in order to contribute to a structured debate on the topic – taking different perspectives and business cases into account.

Standardistion, Innovation, Invention.

I. Introduction

The relation between standardisation and innovation is manifold. Standardisation means a reduction of choice, an agreement on one way of doing things – and thus a decision against alternative ways. Standardisation also means making knowledge public. On the one hand this means that the knowledge is available for others to exploit and built on it. On the other hand it requires the technology owner to contribute his intellectual property which may have taken a lot of time, effort and cost to develop. In other words: in standardisation the technology owner contributes innovation in order to standardise it and via this process to create a base on which others can further innovate.

This paper will elaborate on the complex relations between standardisation and innovation and on how they interrelate to each other. It will look at different aspects of innovation and the role standardisation can play in promoting innovation as well as in providing a way for innovations to get market uptake. On the basis of this analysis some conclusions will be drawn regarding the approach towards standardisation and innovation.

II. Analogy – the cooking stove and the pot

This is trivial, admittedly, but it may help to get a better approach towards the different aspects and quirks of the topic. Everybody who likes cooking spaghetti or asparagus may value the fact that there are special pots which have been designed especially for coping with the length of the respective food. And isn't it nice that whatever pot from whatever producer we buy, it fits onto the hob of the cooking stove. More precisely: the diameter of the pot matches the diameter of the hob. Due to this standardised diameter it is possible for innovators to produce special pots – like the ones for cooking spaghetti and the ones for cooking asparagus – and to successfully offer them on the market place.

How would the alternative situation look like? Imagine the diameter was not standardised. Every producer of cooking stoves would have their own design and measures. They would probably produce pots at the same time and sell the specifically designed pots that fit on each specific model of cooking stove. As a consumer you would be dependent on what this one producer provides you with. And most notably: you would be dependent on the innovation coming from this single producer. And even if the cooking stove producer allowed that others offer pots that match the bods of his various model series it would be very cost intensive for the pot producers to produce a number of different sizes of their pots – all specially designed for the various differing cooking stoves. In consequence, innovation would be slow, depending on some few providers, innovations would most likely not be available pervasively and prices would be high and choice limited.

But there may also be another kind of innovation. The producer of pots, for instance, may have developed a new basic material for making the pots or for surface-coating. He put a lot of R&D efforts into this development and patented the new technology. Now he has two options for bringing it to the market: (i) He can try and establish on the market as the sole producer and vendor and thus try to maximise his competitive advantage; (ii) or he decides to provide the method and technology for the new material to others, as well, e.g. via bringing it into a standard. The second option has the advantage that the new technology is more widely spread and that market acceptance and uptake will be faster. Also marketing cost will be reduced because multiple vendors will promote the new stuff. But the innovator looses his competitive advantage, there is no guarantee that other will not be much more successful in marketing the innovation than he is. So he may at least want to make sure that he gets some reward for the high R&D investment he had put into the development of the new material. The possibility for him to license the patented technology that he brings into the standard and to get some compensation from those who make use of and implement it, is in this scenario both an incentive for bringing innovative technologies into standardisation at all (and thus allowing their broad exploitation) and an incentive for investment in R&D and basic research in general.

III. INNOVATION STRATEGIES

The simplified analogy about the cooking stove and the pots shows that there are different levels of innovation, different mechanisms where and how innovation takes place and how innovation and standardisation interact.

A. Basic Research versus Process and Technology Integration

The common and somewhat traditional way for achieving innovative new products, materials, technologies etc. is by investing into basic research. Depending on the technology area this can often be a very cost and labour intensive, long term investment. And naturally enough not all research activities result in marketable products; some risk of failure is intrinsic to all research activity. Moreover, with basic research the time span from successful research results to marketable products can take quite a long time. This is the well-known elapse time from invention to innovation. This adds on the overall investment and on the risk which companies take for undertaking research activities.

The patent system is one way to make sure that companies are properly rewarded for their research work. Inventions are patented so that a company has the sole right to exploit some innovation for which it has taken long time basic research investment. And it is up to the respective patent owner's discretion whether to allow others to exploit the respective invention as well and use it for innovative products and offers. Is such cases the patent owner grants a license for which, in turn, some royalty-fee is to be paid based on a bilateral license agreement. In this way the patent system provides an incentive to companies to be active in research activities, to invest in basic research, and to strive for inventions and innovation.

But innovation is not limited to basic research and the successful marketing of inventions resulting from basic research. A large amount of innovation also takes place on the level of implementing standards and exploiting the technologies that are available as a standard. In a way this is the very basic idea about standards and standardisation: By defining a standard agreement is reached on the basic technology structures. Competitive differentiation – and thus innovation – takes place on the level of the implementation of the standard. The common standard, in turn, ensures interoperability and choice and prevents customers up to the end-user from single vendor lock-in.

Moreover, today, in Information and Communication Technology, a huge potential for innovation lies in the optimisation of processes, in doing the things that are done more efficiently and smarter. In fact, the term "smart" has meanwhile found its way in a number of topic areas like smart grid, smart home, smart cities, smart commerce, etc. For building such systems, smart technology infrastructures, it is required to integrate different technologies and therefore combine different standards. Interoperability is of key importance here – interoperability enabled via standards. In other words, innovation, innovative new systems and technology integrations, are made possible by the use of standards. Innovation takes again place on the level of the implementation of standards. The availability of standards ensures that technologies can be integrated, that coded information can automatically be processed, so that new services can be offered on top of existing infrastructures.

B. In-house Research versus Collaborative and Open Innovation

A further differentiation regarding innovation can be made considering the way the innovation process is organised. It may be claimed, again, that the traditional way is to invest into research activities in-house. A research department is responsible for finding new features, new substances, new techniques, new products etc. Usually, the respective departments work under considerable security protection because the research results provide the grounds for future competitive differentiation and market success.

With an in-house research approach a company keeps the full control over the research and innovation process. This also means that all potential benefits of inventions can fully be reaped by the respective company, inventions can be patented, and the company has the full decision power of how to exploit the new technologies, methods, etc.

In-house research has often been complemented by specific collaborations, e.g. between a company and one or more university or with guest researchers and similar instruments. This allows a transfer of knowledge while all rules and processes are kept under full control of the collaborating parties.

On a somewhat broader scale knowledge transfer and collaboration are taking place in research consortia where industry – both large and small – and academia get together for doing joint research. This is, most prominently, the case in government funded research projects. A contract or consortium agreement lays down how to deal with the joint research results and also how to tread pre-existing know-how that is brought into the respective project. Usually, there is a mixture between making research results entirely public, sharing them amongst the consortium members only and allowing preferred exploitation for those consortium members who have ownership of the invention.

In addition to the aforementioned well established processes and practices for innovation, the last ten to fifteen years have shown a tendency for increasing collaboration practices and for opening up innovation processes leveraging open innovation. Open innovation can be anything from bi-lateral collaboration of two parties to actual crowd sourcing. The latter is what has significantly changed the innovation landscape in the recent decade. It may well be said that open innovation marks the paradigm shift of the last ten to fifteen years regarding innovation strategy.

The most prominent example for open innovation in ICT are probably open source communities practicing successful collaborative development of software.

Industry largely make use of open innovation and have developed a number of strategies on how to benefit. Some common approaches are
1. Contribute to community managed open source projects, e.g. by providing technologies, expertise and man power; In-house Research versus Collaborative and Open Innovation
2. Create communities and open up technology components for open source development;
3. Donate technologies to open source communities, e.g. for allowing a faster and more broad continuation of development and improvements.

Open innovation and collaboration have shown their benefit to the economy and to society. Their huge potential for driving innovation and progress has been recognised. Along these lines, President Barroso picked up the topic when introducing the overall agenda for his current Commission.. He outlined that, "the application of innovations like Web 2.0 to business and public life is changing the way in which innovation happens. It is becoming more open and collaborative. Once the preserve of a select elite, it now involves a much wider range of actors. [...] crowd-sourcing and co-creation are now the order of the day! We need a new policy that reflects these changes. This means that we will have to, well, innovate!"[1] Concrete examples for projects which the Commission drives to leverage crowd sourcing and open innovation include the open data initiative in the context of public sector information (PSI). By making government data openly available the full potential for innovative use of such data is made open to the public and anybody can access and analyse the data producing some added value results. And in general, governments have realised the potential of open source technologies for the public sector. Open source technologies provide alternatives, but more importantly complement proprietary offerings especially in specialised domains. Following this strategy the European Commission has also set up platforms for sharing technologies, best practices and information around eGovernment software and semantic interoperability: SEMIC.EU and JOINUP which is the successor for OSOR.EU.

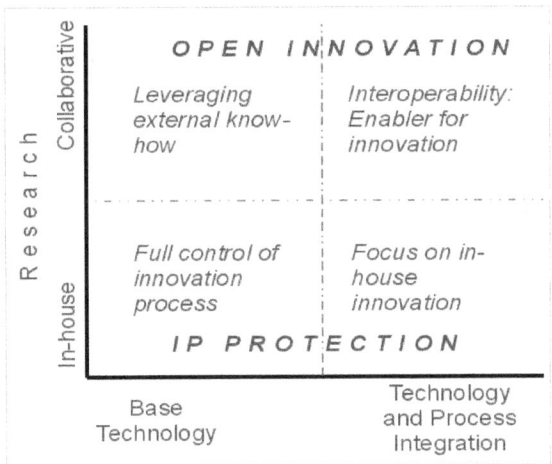

Figure 1: Innovation Matrix

---
[1] Barroso, President of the European Commission, Transforming the EU into an Innovation Society, p. 4.

C. Leveraging the innovation matrix

Probably those companies and players are most successful which leverage all different innovation strategies and most effectively make use of the different strategic options. These can be illustrated in an innovation matrix (Figure 1).

We have two continua or spectra: from in-house research to collaborative research on one angle and from basic research to technology and process integration on the other angle. The more you stay in-house the more you can keep full control over your research work and the innovation cycle and the more you can secure a certain level of IP protection, e.g. for inventions, have full control on filing patents, etc. Collaborative work means opening up the innovation process, entering into exchange with others and leveraging the opportunities of open innovation. This can happen with base technology development; even though it is more likely that collaboration around base technology development focusses on a pivotal exchange of information and know-how, on clearly defined research collaboration, be it bilateral or within some research consortium. But also Linux can be seen as an example for base technology development under the paradigm of open innovation.

The more we move into software, the more do we get at the potential for innovation which lies in the integration of technologies and processes. The innovation process here is a primarily open process combining different services (e.g. in Service Oriented Architectures), driving for competitive offerings, creating added value on top of existing infrastructures. Interoperability is key in this context for ensuring that different modules and technologies work with each other, for ensuring automatic processing of data, for allowing to read data structures and make use of coded information.

One innovation strategy is not better than the other, not more important or promising for the near term future. There may be some areas that can be identified as those with a lot of potential, e.g. because there is some tailback or some area where innovations are now available and therefore get in focus. This is the case for process innovation and technology integration reaping the chances and opportunities that ICT offer for optimisation. In 2006, for instance, the IBM CEO study identified that global CEOs see the highest potential for innovation exactly in this spectrum of integrating processes and technologies. But it was also clearly stated that some focus on process innovation should not mean to neglect other innovation areas: "Business model innovation matters. Competitive pressures have pushed business model innovation much higher than expected on CEOs' priority lists. But its importance does not negate the need to focus on products, services and markets, as well as operational innovation."[2]

In other words, having a proper strategy combining the different approaches to innovation is what matters. As ever so often, there is no "one-size-fits-all" solution, no single route to success, but the mix matters, and it needs to be tailored well to meet the needs and the potential of the respective company and technology developer.

---
[2] Expanding the Innovation Horizon, p. 4.

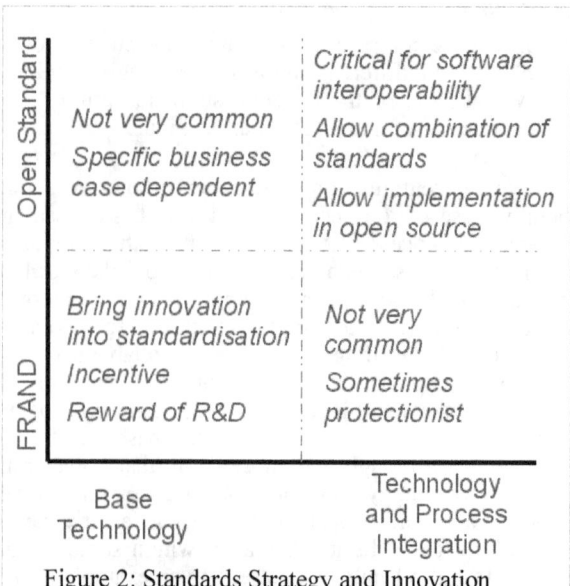

Figure 2: Standards Strategy and Innovation

IV. STANDARDISATION STRATEGIES AND INNOVATION

As we saw in chapters II and III, standardisation can play an important role in innovation and in the innovation process. Standards can play a key role in the transfer of research results and inventions into the market, in making them available for exploitation. But standards also play a role in enabling innovation by providing an agreed and trusted basis on top of which innovation can happen. Figure 2 illustrates this spectrum again in a matrix and outlines the key aspects in the context of strategic considerations regarding standardisation and innovation.

A. From Invention to Innovation

Standardisation can be a way to turn inventions into innovations. The transfer of research results into standardisation makes inventions available for the market and thus can be a tool for bridging the gap between invention and the broad uptake of it which makes it a real innovation.

By bringing new technologies into standardisation they are also made available for exploitation by others. On the one hand a specific innovation gains on market uptake that way and becomes more widespread which can help to create the respective market demand. On the other hand the technology provider owning the respective piece of technology looses his exclusivity by making the invention available to the public via standardisation. He gives up some – potential – competitive advantage. While it is in the interest of the market to have the respective technology available, it carries some risk for the owner.

A common way to reward research activities, minimise the risk for technology providers and provide an incentive to bring new technologies into standardisation is via licensing patent claims that are essential for implementing standards. What is important for standardisation is that the licensing terms and conditions are the same for everyone who wishes to implement that standard. Therefore, standards development bodies lay down that patent rights are available and licensed under FRAND terms and conditions which means they need to be available for everyone under Fair, Reasonable and Non-Discriminatory terms. Patent holders make a commitment to license their patent which is essential for the standard. In return they do get some compensation and thus have an incentive to bring their inventions into standardisaston and via this contribute to innovation.

This system is commonly used in global standardisation and usually works. However, problems occur if there is no agreement on royalty rates, if on party feels that claims are excessive, if certainty on the availability is not there, if there is no clarity on the overall cumulative rate, etc.

This paper is not the place to debate whether FRAND based policies are generally good or bad, nor to discuss the issues that they bring in detail. What is without doubt is the high importance of FRAND based IPR regimes in standardisation for bringing new technologies into standardisation, for promoting the transfer of research results into standards and thus contributing and driving innovation.

However, this is just one aspect of innovation. It works well for base technology work, but has its limitations in areas like software interoperability where license fees and IPR encumbrances can block innovation and be a barrier rather than a facilitator. Moreover, royalty stacking can become a problem to innovation. If in subsequent technology development over the years the number standards that include patents requiring to pay royalty fees reaches a number and a percentage of the overall technology cost that leaves little to no margin to compete and therefore reduces the incentive to add new, innovative technologies.

On a more detailed level amongst specialist for Intellectual Property Rights a number of experiments are being undertaken in how to reduce these issues, how to manage them in a proper was that is agreeable for all parties. Patents pools, ex ante declaration of royalty rights are just two keywords in this context. They address specific issues around the definition and improvement of IPR rules and regimes.

B. Promoting Innovation with Open Standards

Open Standards that are available for implementation and use without restrictions are the prime paradigm for software and information technologies. And they are for the relation between standardisation and innovation in general. The standard provides an agreed basis. Innovation takes place on top of the respective standard, in the implementation and in the actual use of standards. And this is where competitive differentiation occurs: in the use and implementation of standards. Since the standards are available without restrictions, everyone can make use of them and thus everyone can contribute to innovation.

1) The internet and the world wide web

The internet and the world wide web are the prime example of our times showing how open standards have boosted innovation in a remarkable and unprecedented way. The key standards have been available for everyone without cost and Royalty-free. Anybody could – and still can – make use of them, implement them, and thus make use of the internet, provide some new service, new technology – in other words: innovate. And this has led to a number of new business areas, e.g. eBusiness, eCommerce, web shops, automation of processes, process integration, etc.

The leading global standards development bodies around the internet and the world wide web, or better: the stakeholders presend in these standards bodies, agreed that a Royalty-free policy is best suited for the standards that are developed in these organisations which are, in fact, software interoperability standards. They either have clear Royalty-free policies, or options for selecting Royalty-free, or an agreement that internet and web standards should no bear royalties and other licensing restrictions. In this way, standards are not only available for everyone as a basis on which innovation can take place. But the global acceptance and uptake of the respective standards is much facilitated. Usually the respective standard can be downloaded from a website.

It is interoperability between software components which drives innovation in the context of the internet and world wide web. This interoperability is enabled by the use of standards. And the common approach to rely on open standards ensures broad availability of the technologies – including for collaborative development by open source communities.

2) Open Standards and their future potential for innovation

Building on the internet and the world wide web, on the standards infrastructure that is available on the exemplary it has set, there is some significant potential for innovation in the integration of technologies and processes. In order to reap this potential for innovation, open standards are essential to ensure software interoperability and thus to enable that different technology parts and components can be combined, work together and that coded information can automatically be read and processed.

A second area of innovation where Open Standards are critical is Cloud technologies. Only a cloud that builds on open standards will guarantee interoperability and portability. And will ensure that the users, the clients are master of their data. Open standards increase trust, flexibility and duration in a fast changing environment.

3) Systemic standardisation – meta level of standardisation

Technology integration requires the combination of standards into complex systems. This, in turn, implies that the respective standards are identified and selected and that some sort of reference system or reference infrastructure is constructed.

In order to address this issue standards interoperability roadmaps or catalogues have been developed in recent years. These can be seen as meta-standards describing how to successfully realise a specific project by making use and combining standards. Such systemic standardisation projects are often driven by governments that wish to drive innovation in the respective technology areas. Examples from recent years include the highly innovative fields of smart grid and cloud – which both have some strong implication for the public sector as well.

Systemic standardisation recognises the key role of standards in innovation that lies in technology integration. There is, for sure, a high impact regarding which standards are selected, especially if there should be different options from which to choose. Where systemic standardisation aims at creating open ecosystems they lay the ground for further innovation by making use of the reference systems and – yet again – building on top of them, implementing them and differentiating on the implementation level.

V. CONCLUDING REMARKS

This paper has explored the various complexities around invention, innovation and standardisation. There is no single size fits all approach for driving innovation via the use of standards and via standardisation. It is important to consider the full spectrum when defining standardisation and innovation strategies. And also when addressing the topic in a policy context.

There is clearly one area which can be identified where genuinely open standards are essential for facilitating innovation: this is software interoperability. The internet and the world wide web have set the precedent. Open Standards ensure that Open Source technologies can implement them and add to the overall innovation process and innovation cycle. Open Source is a major contributor to innovation and therefore must not be excluded. Leading global IT standards bodies have acknowledged this by implementing respective IPR policies that allow implementation of the standards in Open Source. A royalty-free policy and other licensing terms and conditions that are not imposing further encumbrances are key in software interoperability for promoting further innovation in important growth areas.

LITERATURE

[1] *Barroso, José Manuel Durão (2009), Transforming the EU into an Innovation Society, Speech at the first European Innovation Summit, Brussels, 13 October, 2009. (Available at http://europa.eu/rapid/pressReleasesAction.do?reference=SPEECH/09/478&format=HTML&aged=0&language=EN&guiLanguage=fr).*

[2] *Egyedi, T. (2010): On the implications of competing standards. In: Swedish Competition Authority (Ed.): Pros and Cons of Standard Setting, pp.12-33. Stockholm 2010. Retrieved on 5th July 2012 from: http://www.tbm.tudelft.nl/en/about-faculty/departments/iss-department/ict-section/staff/tineke-m-egyedi/publications/*

[3] *Egyedi, T. (2012): To Select or Not? Dealing with Competing Standards in Public IT Procurement-Final. Research Paper, Delft University of Technology, Delft, Netherlands 2012. Available at http://www.tbm.tudelft.nl/en/about-faculty/departments/iss-department/ict-section/staff/tineke-m-egyedi/publications/*

[4] *Friedrich, J. (2011): Making Innovation Happen: The Role of Standards and Openness in an Innovation-friendly Ecosystem. In: In: Standardization and Innovation in Information Technology (SIIT) 2011 7th International Conference on. Berlin 2011.*

[5] *Openforum Academy (Ed.) (2011): Insights Report - Achieving European Interoperability. Brussels, Belgium. Available at http://www.openforumacademy.org/insights/1102ofa%20insights_report%20interoperability_final.pdf*

[6] *Towards an increased contribution from standardisation to innovation in Europe, Communication from the European Commission to the European Parliament, the Council, the European Economic and Social Committee and the Committee of the Regions, COM(2008) 133, (Available at http://eur-lex.europa.eu/LexUriServ/LexUriServ.do?uri=COM:2008:0133:FIN:en:PDF).*

[7] *Undheim, T. A.; Friedrich, J. (2008): The Momentum of Open Standards - a Pragmatic Approach to Software Interoperability.*

In: European Journal of ePractice No. 5 October 2008. Retrieved on 15th August 2012 from: http://www.epractice.eu/files/5.1.pdf

Openforum Academy

OpenForum Academy is a think tank with a broad aim to examine the paradigm shift towards openness in computing that is currently underway, and to explore how this trend is changing the role of computing in society.

Organisation

OpenForum Academy is an independent programme established by OpenForum Europe. It has created a link with academia in order to provide new input and insight into the key issues which impact the openness of the IT market. Central to the operation of OpenForum Academy are the Fellows, each selected as individual contributors to the work of OFA. A number of academic organisations have agreed to work with OFA, working both with the Fellows and within a network of contributors in support of developing research initiatives.

Supporting the Fellows and Academic organisations are a small Secretariate, led by a Director of Research and Communications , and a Policy Director . The Board of OFE Ltd are responsible for legal and fiscal affairs. A Research Council drives the operation of OFA, formed from Fellows, Academic Partners and the Secretariate.

How to Become a Fellow

Fellows are nominated by the Fellows themselves, and will normally have already exhibited evidence of individual contribution to innovative thinking in the field of IT.

How to Contribute to OFA

New thinking is welcome, and contributions can be submitted for publication on the OFA website and network. Articles should be focussed on the general area of openness within IT. Submissions will be assessed by the Fellows and their decision is final.

OFA Sponsorship

Commercial companies and organisations have the opportunity to be directly associated with the Academy by becoming a Sponsor of the Academy either via support for individual research projects, or core support for the Academy. Preference will be for multiple partners to fund research. However provided the research falls within the remit one industrial partner may fund a research project. Sponsors will be acknowledged in all published material.

OpenForum Academy is the sister organisation to OpenForum Europe, whose mission is "open, competitive choice to the IT user

The Fellows

As of September 2012 the Fellows of OpenForum Academy are:

ALEA FAIRCHILD

ANDREW KATZ

ANDREW UPDEGROVE

ANTHONY D. WILLIAMS

DR. BJORN LUNDELL

BRIAN KAHIN

CAMERON NEYLON

CARLO DAFFARA

CARLO PIANA

CHRIS TAGGART

DR. DANIEL M. GERMAN

DR. EFTHYMIOS ALTSITSIADIS

EMMA MULQUEENY

GEORG GREVE

GLYN MOODY

HELEN DARBISHIRE

DR. JOCHEN FRIEDRICH

DR. JUN IIO

KARSTEN GERLOFF

DR. LAURA DENARDIS

DR. MAHA SHEIKH

DR. PAUL ADAMS

PROF. PETER MURRAY-RUST

PETER SUBER

RUFUS POLLOCK

SHANE COUGHLAN

SIMON PHIPPS

SIMONETTA VEZZOSO

PROF. TETSUO NODA

DR. TINEKE EGYEDI

DR. TONY CORNFORD

TROND-ARNE UNDHEIM

Openforum europe
open, competitive choice for IT users

OpenForum Europe (OFE) is a not-for-profit industry organisation which was originally launched in 2002 to accelerate and broaden the use of Open Source Software (OSS) among businesses, consumers and governments. OFE's role has since evolved and its primary role now is to promote the use of open standards in ICT as a means of achieving full openness and interoperability of computer systems throughout Europe. It continues to promote open source software, as well as openness more generally as part of a vision to facilitate open, competitive choice for IT users.

The OFE Team

Graham Taylor - Chief Executive

Graham Taylor is Chief Executive of OpenForum Europe, and a co-founder of the organisation. A regular speaker at international conferences, he was invited by the European Commission and Portuguese Presidency to respond to the Declaration made at the Ministerial eGovernment Conference in Lisbon in 2007, and succeeded in getting 27 other European organisations from the 'Open Community' to be co-signatories to that Statement.

With some 30 years of experience in the ICT industry, prior to OFE Graham Taylor was a Director at ICL, most recently as Managing Director of the Smart Card business, but with spells as its Software Business Development Manager, and Director of The Solution Centre, ICL's centre for the management of complex integration projects.

Bob Blatchford - Chief Operating Officer

Bob has spent over thirty years in the IT Industry, 23 of them within the insurance sector. Whilst with Lloyd's of London he worked with emerging technologies, cross discipline projects and commercialisation of internal IT services.

Bob has held a number of senior management roles during his career, with responsibility for IT, telecommunications, business development, strategic planning, electronic trading, commercial activities and the development and introduction of Internet based services for markets. He has managed the delivery of a number of successful major projects for the London insurance market.

Bob also has had a long-term involvement and strong interest in the introduction of e-commerce and e-trading initiatives in the London Insurance Market. He was a founding member of both LIMNET (London Insurance Market Network) and LNSG (Lloyd's Network Steering Group) and has been active on a number of national and international committees encouraging and enabling the development of business to business e-commerce and standards.

Basil Cousins – Director and Secretary

Basil Cousins is co-founder and Director of OpenForum Europe (OFE). Over the past two years, he has led the ODF campaign in Europe and is responsible for developing the role of OFE in the UK. A Secretary to the OFE Executive Council and OFE Board, he also provides the secretariat for the highly successful OFE SIGs, Basil has had 40 years experience in the ICT industry.

As DP Manager of Costain, he set up and ran Computel, an ICL based timesharing bureau owned by Costain and Mowlem. As Head of Software Engineering, ICL ASD he was instrumental in the foundation of X/Open and the publication in June 1984 of the first portability guide based on AT&T Unix System V. He then headed up Olivetti UK Public Relations until 1994 when as a member of the CBI London Region Council, he launched LondonLInk in association with Nomura, Lloyds of London, Bird & Bird, Citigroup and others. He is Honorary Secretary of the Ethical Panel of the Information Technologists Panel and Honorary Treasurer of the Real Time Club.

Sachiko Muto - Director

Sachiko Muto joined OFE in 2007 and serves as Director with responsibility for government relations. Sachiko has over ten years of experience working in Brussels public affairs. With degrees in Political Science from the University of Toronto and the London School of Economics, she is currently a guest researcher at TU Delft where she takes an interest in the social and political implications of technological change.

Shane Coughlan - Director

Shane Coughlan is an expert in communication methods and business development. He is best known for building bridges between commercial and non-commercial stakeholders in the technology sector. His professional accomplishments include establishing a legal department for the main NGO promoting Free Software in Europe, building a professional network of over 270 legal counsel and technical experts across 4 continents, and aligning corporate and community interests to launch the first law review dedicated to Free/Open Source Software. Shane has extensive knowledge of Internet technologies, management best practice, community building and Free/Open Source Software. His experience includes engagement with the server, desktop, embedded and mobile telecommunication industries. He does business in Europe, Asia and the Americas, and maintains a broad network of contacts. Shane Coughlan serves as OFE's Director with responsibility for the Far East and additionally acts as the OpenForum Academy Fellow Coordinator.

Members of OpenForum Europe

IBM

Google

ORACLE

Deloitte.

redhat

All Trademarks Belong To Their Respective Companies.

Mission, Policies and Code of Conduct

Introduction OFE pursues the vision of an open, competitive choice for IT users. To that end policies and a Code of Conduct have been adopted in order to:
• define the standards which OFE requires of staff, Council and SIG members;
• make clear to all the high standards with which they will be expected to comply;
• make Governments, Public Sector, Businesses, Consumers, and other Official Bodies aware of the principles and high standards promoted by OFE.

Public Statements

OFE statements will make clear that do not necessary reflect the views of all, or seeks to represent any specific community, nor presents its opinions as being unanimously supported by its full memberships.

Policy

By using effective leadership and management OFE will:
- actively promote the vision to government and business;
- monitor governments positions, support or inform as appropriate;
- set up think tanks to test strategic thinking;
- set up action programmes to implement OFE strategy;
    - standards
    - emerging technology
    - education and training
    - public sector
    - small businesses
- mentor and provide support systems for key influencers;
- identify like minded organisations to network and cooperate;
- establish research programmes to identify issues, audit compliance or monitor uptake;
- take on projects that further the development of the vision.

Code of Conduct

The Code is binding on all OFE staff, Council and SIG members and shall be subscribed to by all as a condition of employment/membership. OFE requires staff, Council and SIG members to: • promote the aims of OFE and conduct themselves in a professional manner so as to reflect credit on OFE;
• use all proper means to promote the mission of OFE and to extend its sphere of influence;
• respect any confidence gained by them from OFE or at Executive Council or SIG meetings;
• make statements or recommendations in a professional capacity objectively and fairly;
• ensure that OFE statements or papers produced by them meet professional standards;
• avoid statements that reflect upon the character or integrity of individuals or organisations;
• carry out their duties equitably in an open and accountable way;
• be polite and supportive in dealing with others, personal abuse is unacceptable.

Useful Links

The OpenForum Europe homepage:

http://www.openforumeurope.org

The OpenForum Academy homepage:

http://www.openforumacademy.org

The OpenForum Academy Fellow Library:

http://www.openforumacademy.org/library/ofa-fellows-reference-library

Further Reading on Openness

These Research links are provided to assist those wanting to investigate Openness issues and have not been endorsed or peer reviewed by OFA or its Fellows, and do not necessarily reflect the organisation's or member's views.

Featured Research

Unlocking Growth, How Open Data Creates New Opportunities for The UK
The report from Deloitte argues that providing data to the public will bring four main benefits.

An Analysis of Open Source Business Models
Open-source software products provide access to the source code [or basic instructions] in addition to executable programs, and allow for this source code to be modified and redistributed. This is a rarity in an industry where software makers zealously guard the source code as intellectual property.

Consortium Info Metalibrary
The Standards <Meta>Library from Consortium Info provides links to almost 1,900 articles relevant to the field of openness.

OFE report shows 21% of public ICT tenders break EU Rules
OFE's annual public procurement monitoring of notices for computer software published on Tenders Electronic Daily results point that non-discrimination on public procurement processes has barely improved from 2008 exercise.

Read more online:
http://www.openforumacademy.org/library/third-party-research

Enter The Conversation

Make your own notes on open innovation.

www.ingramcontent.com/pod-product-compliance
Lightning Source LLC
Chambersburg PA
CBHW080952170526
45158CB00008B/2449